Cana

Travel better, enjoy more

ULYSSES

Travel Guides

OFFICES

Canada: Ulysses Travel Guides, 4176 St. Denis Street, Montréal, Québec, H2W 2M5, ☎(514) 843-9447, Fax: (514) 843-9448, info@ulysses.ca, www.ulyssesguides.com

Europe: Les Guides de Voyage Ulysse SARL, 127 rue Amelot, 75011 Paris, France, ☎01 43 38 89 50, Fax: 01 43 38 89 52, voyage@ulysse.ca, www.ulyssesguides.com

U.S.A.: Ulysses Travel Guides, 305 Madison Avenue, Suite 1166, New York, NY 10165, info@ulysses.ca, www.ulyssesguides.com

DISTRIBUTORS

U.S.A.: Hunter Publishing, 130 Campus Drive, Edison, NJ 08818, ☎800-255-0343, Fax: (732) 417-1744 or 0482, comments@hunterpublishing.com, www.hunterpublishing.com

Canada: Ulysses Travel Guides, 4176 St. Denis Street, Montréal, Québec, H2W 2M5, ☎(514) 843-9882, ext.2232, Fax: 514-843-9448, info@ulysses.ca, www.ulyssesguides.com

Great Britain and Ireland: Roundhouse Publishing, Millstone, Limers Lane, Northam, North Devon, EX39 2RG, ☎1 202 66 54 32, Fax: 1 202 66 62 19, roundhouse.group@ukgateway.net

Other countries: Ulysses Travel Guides, 4176 St. Denis Street, Montréal, Québec, H2W 2M5, ☎(514) 843-9882, ext.2232, Fax: 514-843-9448, info@ulysses.ca, www.ulyssesguides.com

No part of this publication may be reproduced in any form or by any means, including photocopying, without the written permission of the publisher.

Canadian Cataloguing-in-Publication Data (see p 4)
© April 2004, Ulysses Travel Guides.
All rights reserved. Printed in Canada
ISBN 2-89464-720-4

TABLE OF CONTENTS

Author	*Publisher*	*Page Layout*
Pierre Corbeil	André Duchesne	André Duchesne
		Pierre Ledoux
Translation and	*Copy Editing*	
adaptation	Jennifer	*Photography*
Cindy Garayt	McMorran	*Cover page*
	Pierre Daveluy	Patrick Escudero

ACKNOWLEDGEMENTS

We acknowledge the financial support of the Government of Canada through the Book Publishing Industry Development Program (BPIDP) for our publishing activities. We would also like to thank the government of Québec for its SODEC income tax program for book publication.

Canadian Cataloguing-in-Publication Data
Main entry under title :
  Canadian French for better travel
  2nd ed.

  (Ulysses phrase book)
  Includes index.
  Translation of: Le québécois pour mieux voyager
  For English-speaking travellers.
  Text in English and French.

ISBN 2-89464-720-4

1. French language - Conversation and phrase books - English. 2. French language - Provincialisms - Quebec (Province). I. Series.

PC2121.Q4213 2004   448.3'421   C2003-942075-2

INTRODUCTION

Part of what makes travelling fun is getting to hear, speak and learn different languages. Granted, Canada's two official languages, French and English, are not the most exotic of tongues, but the country's rich tapestry of traditions and landscapes has made them unique in their own way.

It goes without saying that French, like all languages, has its own share of nuances and subtleties, not to mention regional variations. These will become more obvious to you as you listen to locals, no matter what province you find yourself in: Québec, the largest French-speaking territory on the globe; Manitoba, home of a strong Franco-Manitoban population; the Maritimes, land of the proud Acadian people, descendants of the first French-speaking settlers in North America, or any other province in the country.

This guide to Canadian French is primarily aimed at English-speakers with some knowledge of French. Although we do touch upon the history and typical expressions of Canada's other francophone regions, this guide mainly focuses on the French that is spoken in the province of Québec. Indeed, this province is the cradle of the French language in Canada and is home to some six-million French speakers.

Some schools have attempted to relegate Québécois French to the status of unnatural by-product, or "poor cousin," of the mother tongue, that is, the French that is spoken in France. But unnatural it is not: Québécois French is its own entity, with its own vocabulary and phonetics. That said, you might be surprised to see that everyday Québécois, whether it is in the workplace, the tourism industry or the media, does not differ that much from "standard" French. To hear the major differences, better turn to Québecois films, songs and literature, as these forms of artistic expression have almost always sought to establish the province's unique linguistic identity. You also may or may not be familiar with the term *joual* (a derivative of *cheval*, meaning "horse"), which designates an inarticulate type, or slang, of Québécois French; this word is still occasionally used but no longer refers to the language in its entirety.

HOW TO USE THIS GUIDE

Most entries in this guide feature three terms or expressions: the first is in Québecois French and is spelled phonetically; the second, in italics, is in "standard" or "international" French; and the third is in English.

Here is a basic pronunciation guide to French:

[a],[à] as in "h**a**t"

[â] as in "f**a**ll"

[é],[er]as in "s**ay**"

[è] as in "**e**very"

[i],[î],[î] as in "tr**ee**"

[o],[ô],[au] as in "g**o**"

[u],[ü] as in "**ü**ber"

[y] as in "tr**ee**" when used on its own; as in "**y**es" when followed by a vowel

[ç] as in "**s**ay"

[ch] as in "**sh**ow"

[gui] as in "**gui**tar"

[oi] as in "**wha**t"

[ou] as in "f**oo**l"

[qui] as in "**ki**wi"

Nasal sounds in French have no direct equivalent in English. Each of the letter combinations used to approximate them is to be treated as a single sound, and the final "n" is never to be heard as a distinct "n." Only by hearing them repeatedly from native speakers will you be able to recognize and reproduce them properly:

[an], [en] as in *v***en***t* or *bl***an***c*

[in] as in *b***ain** or *mat***in**

[eu] as in *d***eu***x* or *f***eu**

[on] as in *garç***on** or *chans***on**

[un] as in *quelqu'***un** or *br***un**

VIVE LA DIFFÉRENCE!

To familiarize you with the particularities of spoken Québécois, this section reveals some of the major distinctions between standard French and Québec French. You could say it is a kind of pronunciation guide, but because you won't necessarily have to produce these sounds to be understood by locals, it is more of a "listening" guide.

Note, however, that the great majority of Québec residents do not limit their language to a jargon that would be incomprehensible to strangers. Most of them can actually switch from an international, impeccable French to a regional, more familiar dialect with great ease. As a result, what you will most often hear in the streets, stores and homes will be a "standard" French punctuated by words and expressions that are typical of the area you're visiting.

CHAMELEON VOWELS

Some of the most distinct, albeit subtle, Québec sounds are those of open vowels that, in international French, are closed: [i], [u] and [ou]. For example:

[i] tends to sound more like [é] (such as the "ay" as in "say"): *péc* instead of *pic*, *créme* instead of *crime*, *légne* instead of *ligne*;

[u] almost sounds like [œ] (such as the "u" in "put"): *jœpe* instead of *jupe*, *pœce* instead of *puce*, *Lœc* instead of *Luc*;

[ou] transforms itself into [au] (such as the "o" in "go"): *saupe* instead of *soupe*, *faule* instead of *foule*, *pausse* instead of *pousse*;

[a] often becomes muted and low at the end of a word, such as the "o" in "bottle." This sound is indicated by [â]: *Canadâ*, *tabâ*;

also at the end of the word, the sound [è] (such as the "e" in "bed") will often sound like [a]: *jam**a*** instead of *jam**ais***, *parf**a*** instead of *parf**ait***, *ba**la*** instead of *bal**let*** or *bal**ai***. This pronunciation can also take place within a word: *m**a**rci* instead of *m**e**rci*.

Another strong difference between European French and Québécois French is the latter's clear distinction between long and short vowels: *p**â**te* and *p**a**tte*; *f**ê**te* and *f**ai**tes*; *j**eû**ne* and *j**eu**ne*; *p**au**me* and *p**o**mme*. In fact, this insistence on long vowels is often exaggerated in familiar speak: *l**aou**che* instead of *l**â**che*, *p**aou**sse* instead of *p**a**sse*, *n**aé**ge* instead of *n**ei**ge*. This also happens in the presence of [r], which elongates a simple, short vowel: *t**aou**rd* instead of *t**a**rd*, *rivi**aé**re* instead of *rivi**è**re* and *enc**aou**re* instead of *enc**o**re*.

Another sound that is really transformed in familiar Québec French is [oi]. It can become [è]: *dr**è**te* instead of *dr**oi**te*, *fr**è**te* instead of *fr**oi**d*; [wé]: *b**wé*** instead of *b**oi**t*, *m**wé*** instead of *m**oi***; [wè]: *b**wè**ter* instead of *b**oi**ter*; [wê]: *déb**wê**ter* instead of *déb**oî**ter*; [wâ]: *b**wâ*** instead of *b**oi**s*; or [waê]: *b**waê**te* instead of *b**oî**te*.

Finally, vowels tend to combine with one another (such as the common *bein*, which sounds like "bain," instead of *bien*) or completely disappear in certain constructions, when even their surrounding consonants evaporate. As a result, you will often hear, especially when listening to a fast speaker, such contractions as ***à'*** *maison* instead of ***à la*** *maison* (in this guide, the apostrophe indicates an elongated sound), and ***sa'*** *rue* instead of ***sur la*** *rue*. You will also hear things like ***y' â*** *dit* instead of ***il lui a*** *dit*, ***twé'*** *zommes* instead of **tous les** *hommes*, or **c'ta inque** *une blague* instead of **c'était rien qu'**une *blague*.

A MENAGERIE OF CONSONANTS

THE BUZZING T AND D

Hearing locals conversing, you may get the eerie feeling that you're standing in the middle of a busy beehive. You will soon discover that this is due to two buzzing consonants: [t] and [d].

Indeed, while these two letters are pronounced more sharply in Europe, in Québécois French they are transformed: [t] becomes [ts] and [d] becomes [dz] before the vowels [i], [u] and [y]. Consequently, you will hear familiar words such as *petit*, *peinture*, *direct*, and *type* become *pe**ts**i*, *pein**ts**ure*, **dz**irect and **ts**ype.

THE ROLLING *R*

The letter [r] can be pronounced in a dozen different ways and is so versatile that it can actually sound different in the mouth of the same speaker, even within a single sentence or word. Indeed, Montréal's inhabitants are still famous for their rolling [r] (which sounds like Spanish), despite the fact that the Québécois standard is gradually opting for the more guttural [r] (which sounds like German).

Other Québécois usually pronounce this letter a bit more "dryly" than Montréalers. In addition, those who favour the more familiar dialect of Québécois will often pronounce the initial [r] of a word

as though it were preceded by the letter [e]: **er**cule instead of
recule, **er**garde instead of **re**garde.

THE FLEEING L

The pronouns il(s) and elle(s) are treated in a most unique way in
Québec French: they actually lose their consonants and can even
be completely transformed.

Therefore, don't be surprised to hear **y** instead of **il** and **ils** (y pârt
demain); **y'â** instead of **il a** (y'â l'intention de venir); and **y'ont** or
y zont instead of **ils ont** (y'ont été bons, y zont été bonnes).

The **elle**, for its part, either turns into **à** (à pârt demain, à l'a
l'intention de venir) or **è** (è bonne, è zont été bonnes).

And as though that weren't complicated enough, the pronoun can
also disappear entirely: sont bons instead of **ils** sont bons, faut faire
ça instead of **il** faut faire ça. The same thing often happens to the
articles la and les, and the prepositions à, dans and sur: j'suis
dans' maison instead of je suis **dans la** maison; j'ai d'l'eau **dins**
yeux instead of j'ai de l'eau **dans les** yeux; mets çâ **sa'** tab' instead
of mets ça **sur la** table.

In the same vein, you may hear the [l], and even the [r] and [t],
fall silent within a word. Here are some examples of this
phenomenon: què'que or even quèk instead of quelque (Voulez-
vous quèk chose?); quéqu'un instead of quelqu'un; mette instead of
mettre (Veux-tu mette çâ lâ?); r'gade or even ga' instead of
regarde (Ga' comme y'é beau!); and dwaêt' instead of doit être.

Introduction

11

THAT NOISY SILENT T

A traditional habit of Québécois French-speakers is to pronounce the final [t] of certain words in which it should be silent. This is especially common in the more familiar dialect: *litte* instead of *lit*; *nuitte* instead of *nuit*; *potte* instead of *pot*, and *boutte* instead of *bout*.

SOUNDS FAMILIAR...

Another characteristic of Québécois French is its strong use of English, as it is peppered with borrowed words and expressions. So much so, in fact, that many of these words have been Gallicised as the years have gone by, and even people who have no knowledge of English use them freely. There may be just as many borrowed expressions in France (*parking*, *pressing*) but in Quebec many are not only borrowed but translated just a little too literally, *fin de semaine* (weekend) is a perfect example. And if you own or rent a car here, don't be surprised by the amount of English you will hear in garages and dealerships: *bréike* (brake), *bréiker* (to brake), *bomm'pœrr* (bumper), *char* (car), *clotche* (clutch), *fla'shœrr* (flasher), *pékope* (pick-up), *troc* (truck), *vanne* (van)... the list goes on and on.

A SELECTION OF ENGLISH WORDS THAT HAVE BEEN ADOPTED BY QUÉBÉCOIS FRENCH

anyway	hot chicken	tune	flocher (to flush)
bill	joke	waiter/waitress	krou'zer (to cruise)
bitch	kick	wiper	
boss	kit	cygne (sink)	ma'tcher (to match)
bullshit	napkin	foqué (fucked)	mou'ver (to move)
business	nerd	pèn'tré (pantry)	
cheap	overtime	smatte (smart)	scâ'rer (to score)
coat	package	tinque (tank)	splitter (to split)
cool	party	toune (tune)	
cute	pizza all-dressed	twisté (twisted)	spotter (to spot)
date	rough	ca'tcher (to catch)	swîtcher (to switch)
deal	safe	clairer (to clear)	
dull	sharp	clî'ner (to clean)	tchèker (to check)
fudge	speech	dî'ler (to deal)	tchopper (to chop)
full	spray	djôker (to joke)	
fun	spring	domper (to dump)	tripper/ badtripper (to trip/bad trip)
game	steady	fitter (to fit)	
goal	stock		troster (to trust)
gravy	straight		
grilled cheese	stuff		
heavy	tight		

Introduction

WHEN GRAMMAR AND
SYNTAX BECOME ONE

DOUBLE YOU

Tsu m'aimes-tsu?, Tsu veux-tsu?, Tsu y penses-tsu?... it seems as though we want to make sure you know we're speaking to you! While standard French dictates that only one pronoun is needed to make a sentence comprehensible, Québécois French often prefers two. To be insistent, extra polite or simply poetic? No one really knows, but one theory claims that this is a deformation of the old Norman dialect. The use of the double *tsu* [tu] is now so common that it has even gone beyond the singular, second-person-pronoun sentence, resulting in such constructions as: *y parle-**tsu**?* instead of *parle-**t-il**?*, *ça s'peut-**tsu**?* instead of *cela se peut-**il**?* and *ch'peux-**tsu*** instead of *puis-**je**?* or *est-ce que **je** peux?*

NO MEANS NO

Despite the fact that standard French grammar insists on indicating the negative with *ne* followed by *pas* or *plus* (such as ***ne** faites **pas** cela* or ***ne** dites **plus** un mot*), many Québécois speakers ignore this rule and drop the *ne*; in their opinion, the *pas* or *plus* is enough to make their intentions clear: *faites pâs çâ; fais pu jamais çâ.*

Here are other examples of common negative-sentence constructions: *oublie pâs d'acheter du lait; y sont pas venus; on aurait pu s'en pâsser.*

ANY QUESTIONS?

To formulate a question in the familiar dialect, all you have to do is repeat an affirmation, preceded by an interrogative word: *Pourquoi tsu fais ça?*; *Comment tsu t'appelles?*... Easy, right?

OTHER UNUSUAL CONSTRUCTIONS TO WATCH OUT FOR:

dis-**mwé-lé** instead of dis-**le moi**

que replacing *dont*: *la fille **que** je t'ai parlé* instead of *la fille **dont** je t'ai parlé*

the prefix *re* that insists on introducing certain words that really don't need it: **re***joindre* instead of *joindre*; **r***entrer* instead of *entrer*; **re***venger* instead of *venger*

the replacement of the verb *devenir* by *venir* (*y'é **venu** tout rouge* instead of *il est **devenu** tout rouge*)

BOY OR GIRL?

While we're on the subject of the unusual, let's discuss another particularity of Québécois French: the apparent "bisexuality" of certain words. Indeed, several of them have been given another gender, as the feminine becomes masculine: **un** *radio*, **un** *tumeur*, **un** *interview*, **un** *moustiquaire*, etc. But the opposite is MUCH more common and is usually seen before a word starting with a vowel or silent h; the adjective or pronoun in these cases is feminine and so the word becomes so as well: **une** *grosse appétit*, **une** *grosse accident*, **une** *grosse orage*, **une** *grande orchestre*, **la** *grosse orteil*, **une** *belle âge*, **une** *autobus*, **une** *hôpital*, **une** *job*, **une** *sandwich*, **une** *belle avion*, *de* **la** *jute*, *de* **la** *bonne argent*, *de* **la** *belle ouvrage*... we've come a long way, baby!

Introduction

15

A BIT OF HISTORY

QUÉBÉCOIS FRENCH

French colonization of Québec dates back to the early 17th century. Contrary to popular belief, the first settlers of New France were not idle, illiterate peasants but rather (for the most part) educated artisans and labourers from urban regions such as Poitou and Normandy. This is actually quite remarkable since the illiteracy rate in France in those days was approximately 80%. In addition, the settlers were accustomed to high society and were familiar with "central" French — the language of administration — even though they spoke their own regional dialects. French villages of that era featured countless dialects.

In the settlement's early days, "a wide array of dialects coexisted. Those that greatly differed from French, to the point of hindering communication, were doomed to extinction, while those that resembled it enough to make communication possible were maintained by their speakers" (R. Mougeon and É. Beniak, *Les origines du français québécois*, Presses de l'Université Laval, 1994; our translation). Norman dialects had the most marked impact on Québécois French; they are the source of several Canadian terms and expressions.

Furthermore, the very nature of the colony, whose development required a multitude of social and commercial interactions between settlers originating from different regions of France, soon resulted in an unusual cohesion and convergence of language. Consequently, it wasn't long before Québec had a strongly unified language that was much less variable than it was in the motherland. This standardization, which occurred in the late 17th century, apparently followed the lines of conventional French, which was spoken by the colony's elite but also, and perhaps especially, by most women who had settled in the New World. These women educated their children in French and therefore played a key role in establishing the language.

Still, a number of terms and pronunciations fiercely resisted the systematic alignment to normalized French. Gradually, additional regionalisms appeared throughout the entire Québec territory and survive to this day. Obviously, as soon as a diverse French population began to develop miles away from the old country, confronting realities and requirements that were very different from its past experience, its language headed in a new direction. In addition, since quick and efficient means of communication would not be created for another two centuries, the decisions and choices made on one side of the ocean took quite a while to reach the other.

Other factors explain certain fundamental digressions in the 18th and 19th centuries between Québécois French and "central" French, particularly in terms of grammatical constructions. Early New France had very few schools and little access to the written word, since books were rare, as were other printed text (notices, signs, etc.) in the rural areas where most settlers lived. As a result, many "intuitive" constructions, much like the ones that emanate from the mouths of children, spread freely and, in some places, left an indelible mark.

We cannot ignore the contribution of Aboriginal peoples who, having inhabited the country well before the French, had already named many places, animals, plants and dishes. The English, who wasted no time following the French to the Canadian territory,

Introduction

also left a legacy that is still quite evident in Québécois French. In fact, the conquest of New France by Britain in 1759 severed Québec's ties to France and to European French so dramatically that French Canada did not directly take part in the evolution of European French for nearly two centuries. During this time, the French language in Canada lived side by side with English, borrowing from its commercial and technical vocabulary. Today, the province's eight-million inhabitants are surrounded by some 300-million English speakers living in the United States and the rest of Canada. With its rich past and proud people, this resilient language is a true survivor.

ACADIAN FRENCH

"Acadian French" designates the variety of French that is spoken in Canada's Atlantic provinces. It differs not only from "standard" French but also from all other dialects spoken in Canada, which all resemble Québécois.

The first Acadian settlers travelled from all corners of France but were mostly from the country's western region. Today, nearly half of all Acadians can trace their roots to that area, which is why there are major differences between Québécois and Acadian French; indeed, less than a third of all Québécois came from western France.

Several factors influenced the development of Acadian French. In 1710, the British seized Acadia from the French, renamed it Nova Scotia and founded Halifax in 1749. A few years later, Governor Charles Lawrence ordered what he believed to be a preventive measure: the deportation of Acadians he suspected were still faithful to France and therefore posed a threat of rebellion. Three quarters of the population were deported and the rest fled. Upon their return several years later, they became geographically isolated, lacked linguistic rights and were surrounded by hostile English speakers, but they were able to prevent assimilation by forming French-speaking enclaves throughout the Atlantic provinces. The distance between these small communities, however, and their minority situation in a sea of anglophones, created many differences within Acadian French itself. It is interesting to note that these dialectical varieties do not correspond to provincial borders or city limits but rather to generations and socio-economic realities.

The province of New Brunswick boasts several regional dialects. In the northern region, the proximity of Québec has resulted in a strong influence of Québécois French and the use of English terms is rather limited. In the south, however, the situation is different: it is said that the French spoken here is the most representative of Acadian French. It is composed of two dialects: the first is traditional and the second, known as *chiac*, is spoken by younger Acadians. *Chiac* is the result of close contact with the anglophone community, especially in the urban setting of Moncton, and combines French, English and "old French." More than anywhere else in Acadia, switching from French to English and vice versa while conversing is quite common here.

Contrary to the province of Québec, Acadians do not have the legal power to protect their language. It is subjected to four different provincial jurisdictions (New Brunswick, Nova Scotia, Prince Edward Island, and, to a lesser extent, Newfoundland and Labrador), even though the majority of the Acadian community, some 250,000 inhabitants, lives in New Brunswick. Today, French

Introduction

speakers represent over 20% of the total Atlantic population; in New Brunswick, that number rises to 34%.

THE REST OF CANADA

ONTARIO

The French presence in Ontario dates back some 350 years, with the establishment of Catholic missions in 1649 and 1742. Around 1880, francophones settled in the heart of the province, then in the northern regions in the early 20th century. Over the last 40 years, Ontario's francophone community has been enriched by the arrival of francophones from Europe, the West Indies, Asia and Africa.

Today, Ontario's francophone community numbers 542,000, representing 5% of the province's population. Although French speakers are scattered throughout Ontario, the eastern part of the province is where most have chosen to live. Ontario has over 350 French elementary and secondary schools, two bilingual universities, two bilingual university colleges and three francophone community colleges.

THE PRAIRIES AND WESTERN CANADA

French-Canadian "Voyageurs" from Lower Canada came to this region in the 18th century, having followed the route mapped by the explorer La Vérendrye. Many of them married Aboriginal women, and their children became known as the Metis. French continued to be the language of the Roman Catholic clergy after its arrival at the Red River Colony in 1818, and its capital,

St. Boniface, is still the francophone hub of Manitoba. Several decades later, francophones arrived from Québec and New England, as well as France, Belgium and Switzerland. Although they are small, the French-speaking communities of these provinces are alive and well, boasting French-speaking associations, community centres, schools, businesses, television and radio stations, and newspapers.

Manitoba's francophones represent less than 5% of the provincial population. The official status of the French language in Manitoba was re-established in 1979 and Franco-Manitoban school governance was won in 1993.

In Saskatchewan, the Fransaskois community is scattered north of Saskatoon and south of Regina. In 1968, francophones' rights to education in French were recognized, and in 1993, they were given authority to administer their own schools.

For its part, Alberta's francophones number approximately 60,000 and are scattered throughout the entire province. The French fur-traders and missionaries were the first to settle parts of Northern Alberta and towns like Rivière-qui-Barre, St-Paul and St-Albert are a testament to the French presence. Here, there are 20 French-language schools and several bilingual college and university programs.

In 1793, six French-Canadians travelled with Alexander Mackenzie to British Columbia and francophones settled permanently, eventually outnumbering anglophones. However, the gold rush at the end of the 19th century brought so many immigrants that they became a minority. In 1909, the small francophone community of Maillardville was founded, but it was only in 1996

Introduction

that Franco-Columbians officially formed a French-language school board.

THE NORTH

As they did in the West and North, francophones came to the Yukon Territory with the fur trade and the Catholic missions. Today, the population of the Yukon barely exceeds 31,000 people, about 4% of whom speak French.

There was a French presence as early as 1665 in the present-day Northwest Territories, as Pierre-Esprit Radisson and Médart Chouart, known as Des Groseillers, were responsible for founding the Hudson's Bay Company in 1670. The first non-Aboriginal person to reach Great Slave Lake was Laurent Leroux, a francophone. In 1786, he established the Fort Resolution trading post and, in 1789, he and other francophones accompanied Alexander Mackenzie on their Mackenzie River expedition.

The 19th century brought European missions; francophones made up half the population, the other half being Aboriginal peoples. Francophones here, who number about 1,000, must fight to preseve their culture. In 1984, the Government of the Northwest Territories passed legislation conferring official language status on eight languages, including French.

In 1999, 60% of the Northwest Territories' eastern corner officially became the territory of Nunavut, "our land" in Inuktitut. This new Canadian territory counts a French-speaking population of approximately 800 people.

FREQUENTLY USED WORDS AND EXPRESSIONS

Oui/Oué
Oui
Yes

Non
Non
No

Bonjour.
Bonjour./Au revoir.
Hello./Goodbye.

Merci/Merci, là.
Merci.
Thank you.

Bienvenue.
Je vous en prie./De rien.
You're welcome.

S'cuze./S'cuze-mwé.
Excuse-moi.
Excuse me.

Comment tsu t'appelles?
Comment t'appelles-tu?
What's your name?

**Mon nom est Daniel./Mwé, mon nom, cé Daniel.
(Moi, mon nom, c'est Daniel.)**
Je m'appelle Daniel.
My name is Daniel.

Comment ça vâ?
Comment allez-vous?
How are you?

Bien, merci.
Bien, merci.
Fine, thank you.

Comme sur des roulettes.
Tout baigne dans l'huile.
Couldn't be better.

bein/don bein
bien/beaucoup/très
good/a lot/very

cou'don (Écoute-donc)
puisque c'est comme ça/dis donc
oh, well

d'abord
dans ce cas
in that case

en tout câs/en té câs/en twé câs (En tous les cas)
quoi qu'il en soit
anyway/no matter what happens

fa que (fait que)/ça fa que
alors/cela fait que
so/therefore

mettons
disons
let's say

pantoute/pas pantoute
du tout/pas du tout
not at all

wa'ein
Ouais
yeah

Frequently Used Words and Expressions

Ça vâ tsu bein?
Êtes-vous bien?/Est-ce que ça fonctionne bien?/Est-ce que tout se déroule comme prévu?
Are you okay?/It it working properly?/Is everything going according to plan?

Y'en a don bein!
Il y en a vraiment beaucoup!
There's so much!

Y'é don bein susceptible!
Ce qu'il peut être susceptible!
He's so touchy!

Ç't'épouvantable!/Ç't'effrayant!/Çé bein effrayant!
Vous m'en direz tant!/Cela n'a aucun sens!/C'est incroyable!/C'est inacceptable!/C'est révoltant!
You don't say!/That makes no sense!/That's incredible!/That's unacceptable!/That's revolting!

Bein cou'don...
Eh bien, puisque c'est comme ça...
Oh, well, if that's the way it has to be...

Cou'don (écoute donc), é tsu malade?
Dis donc, es-tu malade?
Tell me, are you crazy?

26

OK, d'abord.
D'accord.
Okay then.

Ch'te l'dzi pâs, d'abord.
Puisque c'est comme ça, je ne te le dis pas.
If that's the way it's going to be, I won't tell you.

OÙ - OÙ Ç'QUE (WHERE)

Où ç'que cé?	*Où est-ce?*	Where is it?
Où ç'qu'y é?	*Où est-il?*	Where is he?
Où ç'qu'à lé?	*Où est-elle?*	Where is she?
Où ç'qu'y sont?	*Où sont-ils?*	Where are they?

Où ç'qu'y'é votre hôtel?
Où se trouve votre hôtel?
Where is your hotel?

Deyoù (d'où) ç'que té?
Où es-tu?
Where are you?

D'où ç'que vous venez?
D'où venez-vous?
Where are you from?

Frequently Used Words and Expressions

Où ç'tsu t'en vas, d'même?
Où vas-tu comme cela?
Where are you going like that?

icitte/icid'ans	*ici*	here
à drète	*à droite*	to the right
tout drète	*tout droit*	straight ahead
en d'sour	*sous/ en dessous*	under/ underneath
monter en haut	*monter*	to go up
descendre en bas	*descendre*	to go down/ to descend

Ç'tsu loin d'icitte?/Ç'tsu proche d'icitte?
Est-ce loin d'ici?/Est-ce près d'ici?
Is it far from here?/Is it nearby?

Y fa don bein frette icid'ans!
Ce qu'il peut faire froid ici! (à l'intérieur)
Boy, it's really cold in here!

Ergarde en d'sour de la table.
Regarde sous la table.
Look under the table.

Frequently Used Words and Expressions

QUOI - QU'ESSÉ/QU'ESS (WHAT)

qu'essé
qu'est-ce que
what

Qu'ess-tsu veux?/Qu'essé qu'tsu veux?
Que veux-tu?
What do you want?

Qu'ess ça veut dire?/Qu'ess ça veut dire, çâ?
Qu'est-ce que ça signifie?/Que voulez-vous dire par là? /Quelle bêtise as-tu donc faite là?/Mais pourquoi me dis-tu ça?
What does this mean?/What do you mean by that?/What have you done?/Why are you telling me this?

COMMENT/COMBIEN - COMMENT-Ç'QUE (HOW/HOW MUCH)

Comment-ç'que cé chez vous?
Comment est-ce chez vous?
What's it like where you live?

Comment-ç'qu'y vâ ton frère?
Comment va ton frère?
How's your brother?

Comment-ç'qu'y était vot guide?
Comment avez-vous aimé votre guide?
How did you like your guide?

Comment-ç'qu'y font pour faire çâ?
Comment s'y prennent-ils pour faire cela?
How do they do it?

Comment-ç'qu'y sont?
Combien sont-ils?
How many are they?

Comment ça coûte?/Comment-ç'que ça coûte?
Combien cela coûte-t-il?
How much does it cost?

Ç'tsu cher?/Ç'pâs cher.
Est-ce cher?/Ce n'est pas cher.
Is it expensive?/It's not expensive.

Ç'pâs donné.
Ce n'est pas donné.
It's not cheap.

Çé bein cher!
Comme c'est cher!
That's really expensive!

Ça coûte les yeux d'la tête!
Ça coûte une fortune!
It costs an arm and a leg!

Quand çé qu'on y vâ?/Quant'ess qu'on y vâ?/Quant'ess que (quand est-ce que) cé qu'on y vâ?
Quand y allons-nous?/Quand partons-nous?
When are we going?

t'suite/tsu suite	*tout de suite*	right now/ right away
asteure	*maintenant/ de nos jours*	now/ these days
à matin	*ce matin*	this morning
à swèr	*ce soir*	tonight/ this evening

Quel jour qu'on é?
Quel jour sommes-nous?
What day is it?

Quelle heure qu'y'é?
Quelle heure est-il?
What time is it?

Y'é ts'une heure.
Il est une heure.
It's one o'clock.

Frequently Used Words and Expressions

Y'é twâ zeures.
Il est trois heures.
It's three o'clock.

Une meunutte (minute), si vous pla.
Un instant, s'il vous plaît.
One moment, please.

'Tends meunutte.
Un instant.
Wait a minute./Hold on.

EST-CE/N'EST-CE PAS - Ç'TSU (IS IT/ISN'T IT)

Ç'tsu (c'est-tu) loin?
Est-ce loin?
Is it far?

Ç'tsu assez?
Est-ce suffisant?
Is it enough?

Ç'tsu plate, yinqu'in (rien qu'un) peu!
Comme c'est navrant/ennuyeux!
This is so boring!/What a shame!

Frequently Used Words and Expressions

Ç't'au (c'est au) boutte!
C'est vraiment formidable!
This is fantastic!

Ç'tsu çâ qu'vous avez d'mandé?
Est-là ce que vous avez demandé?
Is this what you asked for?

Ç'tsu assez fort?
N'est-ce pas extraordinaire?/
Le volume de la musique est-il suffisamment élevé?/
La teneur en alcool de ton cocktail est-elle suffisante?
Isn't it great?/
Is the music loud enough?/
Is your cocktail strong enough?

Mets-en!
À qui le dis-tu?
You bet!/You can say that again!

JE, TU, IL/ELLE... (I, YOU, HE/SHE...)

chu/ch'	*je suis*	I am
mwé	*moi*	I/me
mwé avec/ mwé'si/mwé itou/ mwé'tou	*moi aussi*	me too
twé	*toi*	you
t'sé/t'sé, lâ	*tu sais*	you know

Frequently Used Words and Expressions

nous autres/nouzô'te	*nous*	us/we
vous autres/vouzô'te	*vous*	you (plural)
eux autres/euzô'te	*ils, elles*	them

Ch'sé pâs./Ch'é pâs.
Je ne sais pas.
I don't know.

Ch'pâs capab/Chu pâs capab de...
Je ne suis pas capable/Je suis incapable de...
I can't/I am unable to...

Ch'pal pâs anglais.
Je ne parle pas l'anglais.
I don't speak English.

Ch'peux-tsu avoir/awêr...?/Ch'pourrè-tsu avoir/awêr...?
Puis-je avoir...?/Pourrais-je avoir...?
May I have...?/Could I have...?

Ch'peux-tsu à' voir/à' wèr?
Puis-je la voir?
May I see her?

Ch'comprends pâs ç'que vous dzites.
Je ne comprends pas ce que vous dites.
I don't understand what you're saying.

Ch'comprends!
Tu parles!/À qui le dites-vous!
I'll say!/You can say that again!

1 3 5

2 4 6

7 8 9

NUMBERS

twâ	*trois*	three
kat	*quatre*	four
cein fois	*cinq fois*	five times
vingt-cein cennes	*vingt-cinq cents*	twenty-five cents/a quarter
si'chaises	*six chaises*	six chairs
sè'piasses	*sept piastres (dollars)*	seven dollars
ne' places	*neuf places*	nine spots/places
s'sante-twâ	*soixante-trois*	sixty-three
s'sante-diss/ s'sante et diss	*soixante-dix*	seventy

WEIGHTS AND MEASURES

Although Canada has been officially using the Metric system since 1970, many people (especially those who were born before that year) still use the old Imperial system.

pouce	inch	(1 in=2.5 cm)
pied	foot	(1 ft=30cm)
verge	yard	(1 yd=0.9m)
mille	mile	(1 mi= 1.6km)
once	ounce	(1 oz=28g)
livre	pound	(1 lb=454g)
demiard	half-pint	(1 half-pint=0.25L)
chopine	pint	(1 pint=0.5L)
pinte	quart	(1 Imperial quart= 1.1L)
gallon	gallon	(1 Imperial gallon=4.5L)
acre	acre	(1 acre=0.4ha)

accotoir/accotwêr
accoudoir
armrest

barouetter
brasser/secouer
to be carried/to be shaken

châr
voiture
car

kat-par-kat
VTT
four-wheel-drive vehicle

dix-huit-roues
semi-remorque
eighteen-wheeler

route pavée
route revêtue
paved road

chemin de garnotte
chemin de gravier
gravel road

flaïyer (flagger, caller) un taxi
héler un taxi au passage
to hail a cab

On s'é faite barouetter su'un vrai temps.
Nous avons été amplement secoués.
We were really shaken up.

THE CAR

In Canadian French, many words relating to cars and driving are borrowed from English. You will find a few on this list.

bréïke	*frein*	brake
bréïke à brâs	*frein à main*	handbrake
bréïker	*freiner*	to brake
cap de roue	*enjoliveur*	hub cap
chauffer	*conduire*	to drive
chaufferette	*système de chauffage*	heater
cramper	*braquer ses roues*	to turn the steering wheel

débarquer	*descendre (d'un véhicule)*	to get out/off (a vehicle)
écarté	*perdu*	lost

embarquer
monter (dans un véhicule)
to get in/climb aboard (a vehicle)

flaïyer	*aller vite*	to go very fast
fla'sher	*clignoter*	to flash/to signal
frapper	*happer/ renverser/ heurter/emboutir*	to hit/ to bump into
gâz/gâzeline	*essence*	gas
hautes	*feux de route/ phares*	high beams
lumière	*feu*	traffic light
millage	*kilométrage*	mileage
minoune	*vieux tacot/bagnole*	old car
miroir	*rétroviseur*	mirror
parcomètre	*parcmètre*	parking meter
remorqueuse	*dépanneuse*	tow truck
scraper	*bousiller*	to wreck ("to scrap")
tinquer	*faire le plein*	to fuel up ("tank up")
valise	*coffre*	trunk

Transportation

virer/erviror *tourner* to turn

vitre/vitte *glace/* window/
pare-brise windshield

zone de touage/remorquage
zone d'enlèvement des véhicules en infraction
towing zone

Y chauffe bein mal!
Ce qu'il conduit mal!
What a terrible driver!

Vâ falwêr chauffer le châr avant d'partir.
Il va falloir réchauffer la voiture avant de partir.
We'll have to warm up the car before leaving.

Crampe en masse.
Braque tes roues à fond.
Put on the hand brake.

On â embarqué deux pousseux (viens de "pouce").
Nous avons fait monter deux auto-stoppeurs.
We picked up two hitchhikers.

On les â débarqués au coin.
Nous les avons fait descendre de voiture à l'intersection.
We dropped them off at the corner.

T'as-tsu bârré ta porte?
As-tu verrouillé ta portière?
Did you lock the (car) door?

Vous vous êtes pâs écartés pantoute?
Vous ne vous êtes pas égarés du tout?
You didn't get lost at all?

On é resté djammés dans l'traffic.
Nous avons été pris dans la circulation.
We got stuck in traffic.

On â frappé une bwête à lett' sans faire eksiprès.
Nous avons heurté une boîte aux lettres sans le faire exprès.
We accidentally hit a mailbox.

Pèse su'l gâz.
Appuie sur l'accélérateur.
Step on the gas.

Ça slaïye au boutte.
Ça glisse énormément.
It's very slippery.

Tchèke dé deux bords avant d'passer.
Regarde des deux côtés avant de passer.
Look both ways before crossing.

Transportation

La tinque é bein pleine.
Le réservoir est bien plein.
The gas tank is full.

Tasse-twé!
Range-toi!/Laisse-moi passer!
Get out of the way!/Let me through!

On é rendus.
Nous sommes arrivés.
We're here.

**Y faisait nwêr comme su'l'yâb (sur le diable)/
comme chez l'loup.**
Il faisait nuit noire.
It was dark as night.

pâsser sa' rouge
griller un feu rouge
to run a red light

une police/un châr de police
une voiture de police
a police car

souffler dans' baloune
souffler dans l'ivressomètre/passer l'alcootest
to take a Breathalyzer

pogner un tickèt
attraper une contravention
to get a ticket

GETTING THERE

bas de la ville	*centre-ville*	downtown
coin	*angle*	corner
lumière	*feu de circulation*	traffic light
pancarte	*enseigne/ affiche/panneau*	sign

Faites le tour du bloc.
Contournez le quadrilatère./Faites le tour du pâté de maison.
Go around the block.

Ç'ta deux coins d'rue d'ici.
C'est à deux rues d'ici.
It's two blocks from here.

Tourne à drwète à'lumière/aux lumières.
Tourne à droite au(x) feu(x) de circulation.
Turn right at the (traffic) lights.

Çé marqué sa' pancarte.
C'est écrit sur le panneau.
It's written on the sign.

Transportation

Vous êtes kèzman (quasiment) rendu.
Vous êtes presque arrivé.
You're almost there.

MONEY

piasse/huard
dollar
dollar/loony

un trente sous/un vingt-cein cennes
une pièce de 25 cents
a quarter

un dzi cennes
une pièce de 10 cents
a dime

un cein cennes
une pièce de 5 cents
a nickel

une cenne/une cenne noire
une pièce de 1 cent
a penny

bidou
argent/billet /dollar
money/bill/dollar

flô'ber
dépenser à tort et à travers
to spend carelessly

gratteux	*avare/économe*	miser
ménager	*faire des économies*	to save money
passer	*prêter*	to lend
séraphin	*avare*	scrooge
tsiper	*laisser un pourboire*	to tip

Changer kat trente sous pour une piasse.
On ne gagne rien au change.
It's six of one and half a dozen of the other.

TELECOMMUNICATIONS

malle	*courrier*	mail
maller	*poster*	to mail
signaler	*composer*	to dial/to call
engagé	*occupé*	busy
charges renversées	*frais virés*	collect call

La malle es-tsu passée?
A-t-on livré le courrier?/Le facteur est-il passé?
Did the mail come?

T'â yeinqu'à (rien qu'à) appeler le 411.
Tu n'as qu'à t'adresser aux renseignements.
Just dial 411.

ELECTRICITY

fil	*cordon électrique*	electric wire
jus	*courant*	power/"juice"
lumière	*ampoule*	light bulb
plogue	*prise de courant/ fiche*	electrical outlet/ plug
ploguer	*brancher*	to plug in

La lumière d'wêt' brûlée.
L'ampoule doit être grillée.
The light bulb must have blown.

THE WEATHER

bordée de neige
forte chute de neige
heavy snowfall

breumasser
pleuvoir très finement
light drizzle

Practical Information

caler dans' bwette
s'enfoncer dans la boue
to sink in mud

caler dans' neige
s'enfoncer dans la neige
to sink in snow

coat d'pwèle/d'chat
manteau de fourrure
fur coat

cass de pwèle
chapeau de poil
fur hat

déhors/dewâors/dwâors
dehors/à l'extérieur
outside

frette	*froid*	cold
geler	*avoir froid*	to be cold
mouiller	*pleuvoir*	to rain
pogné dans' neige	*pris dans la neige*	stuck in snow
poudrerie	*neige chassée par le vent*	drifting snow

renfoncer	*s'enfoncer*	to sink
tempête de neige	*importante chute de neige*	snowstorm

banc de neige
amas de neige entassée par le vent ou à la suite d'un déblaiement
snowbank

charrue
chasse-neige motorisé
snowplow

souffleuse
appareil motorisé qui projette la neige au loin
snow blower

Y mouille-tsu?
Est-ce qu'il pleut?
Is it raining?

Y mouille à sieau./Y tombe des clous./Y pleut à boire debout/à bwêr deboutte.
Il pleut très abondamment.
It's raining cats and dogs.

Y fa frette!
Il fait un de ses froids.
It's very cold.

Y'en â tombé une shotte!/ On'n'â eu toute une bordée!
Il a vraiment beaucoup plu/neigé.
A lot of rain/snow fell.

Ça cale./Ça renfonce.
Le sol est mou/La neige est molle, de sorte qu'on y enfonce.
The ground/snow is so soft you sink through it.

Y fa tsu assez beau dwâors?
Ne fait-il pas un temps superbe?
Isn't it beautiful outside?

Y fa trop frette pour se promener la falle à l'air.
Il fait trop froid pour sortir le cou à l'air.
It's too cold to go outside without a scarf.

Ermonte le chauffage, on gèle.
Mets plus de chauffage, nous avons froid.
Turn up the heat; we're freezing.

OUTDOORS

OUTDOOR ACTIVITIES

bécyk	*vélo/bicyclette*	bicycle
bécyk à twâ roues	*tricycle*	tricycle
chaloupe	*barque*	rowboat
crèmer	*enduire de crème solaire*	to apply sunscreen
gougounes	*sandales de plage*	flip-flops
marche	*promenade à pied*	walk
moineau de badminton	*volant de badminton*	shuttlecock/birdie
noirceur/nwêrceur	*obscurité/nuit tombée*	darkness
plemer	*peler*	to peel (skin)
traîne-sauvage	*toboggan*	toboggan

Ch'te dzi qu'y'â un maudzi beau bécyk!
Il a vraiment un très beau vélo!
He has a really beautiful bicycle!

On vâ-tsu prendre une marche?
Ça te dirait d'aller faire une promenade?
Would you like take a walk?

FAUNA

achigan	*perche noire*	bass
barbotte	*poisson-chat*	catfish
bébitte à patates	*coccinelle*	ladybug
bébitte/bibitte	*insecte*	bug
chevreuil	*cerf d'Amérique*	deer
doré	*poisson d'eau douce*	yellow pike
écureux	*écureuil*	squirrel
joual/jouaux	*cheval/chevaux*	horse/horses
maringouin	*moustique*	mosquito
maskinongé	*brochet géant*	pike
mouche à chevreuil	*petit taon*	deerfly
mouche à cheval	*grosse mouche piquante*	horsefly
orignal	*grand cerf d'Amérique*	moose

ouananiche	*saumon d'eau douce*	lake trout
ouâouâron	*grenouille géante*	bull frog
pic-bois	*pic/pivert*	(green) woodpecker
siffleux	*marmotte*	marmot/ groundhog
suisse	*tamia/écureuil rayé*	chipmunk
p'tsi pwèssons dé ch'naux	*petits poissons des chenaux*	Atlantic tomcod or Tommy cod

CREATURE COMFORTS

LODGING AND THE HOME

air climatisé	*air conditionné*	air conditioner/ air conditioning
bârrer	*verrouiller/ fermer à clé*	to lock
bloc/ bloc appartement	*immeuble résidentiel*	apartment building
câdre	*tableau*	painting
calorifère	*radiateur*	radiator
canal	*chaîne de télévision*	television channel
cave	*sous-sol*	basement
chaise berçante	*berceuse*	rocking chair
châssis	*fenêtre*	window
côloc	*colocataire*	roommate
coquerelle	*cafard/blatte*	cockroach
coqueron	*placard/ très petite pièce*	hole in the wall/small room
fournaise	*chauffage central*	furnace
galerie	*balcon*	balcony
garde-robe	*placard*	closet
pôle	*tringle*	curtain rod
portique	*hall d'entrée*	entrance hall
poste	*chaîne de télévision*	television channel

prélart	*linoléum*	linoleum
support	*cintre*	hanger
tévé	*télévision*	television
vidanges	*ordures/déchets*	garbage

Vous z'avez pas mis l'air climatisé?
Vous n'avez pas fait fonctionner l'air conditionné?
You didn't turn on the air conditioning?

Y ress dans un bloc.
Il habite un immeuble résidentiel.
He lives in an apartment building.

Y'ont une maudzite belle cabane.
Ils ont une maison vraiment magnifique.
They have a really beautiful house.

Si vous avez frette, on peut vous rajouter un calorifère.
*Si vous avez froid, nous pouvons vous procurer
un radiateur d'appoint.*
If you're cold, we can get you an extra heater.

Laissez pas traîner d'manger
si vous voulez pâs attirer é'coquerelles.
*Ne laissez traîner aucune nourriture si vous ne voulez
pas attirer les cafards.*
Don't leave any food out if you don't want to
attract cockroaches.

Creature Comforts

Y'â tsu assez d'supports dans l'garde-robe?
Y a-t-il suffisamment de cintres dans le placard?
Are there enough hangers in the closet?

Quand t'y fa beau, on veille sa' galerie.
Quand le temps est doux, nous passons la soirée sur le balcon.
When it's nice out, we spend the evening on the balcony.

Les vidanges passent le mardi pi l'jeudi.
La cueillette des ordures se fait le mardi et le jeudi.
The garbage is collected on Tuesday and Thursday.

THE BEDROOM

bureau	*commode*	chest of drawers
cadran	*réveille-matin*	alarm clock
couverte/couvarte	*couverture*	blanket
couvre-pieds	*couvre-lit*	bedspread
douillette	*duvet/couette*	comforter/ quilt/duvet
robe de chambre	*peignoir*	bathrobe

Creature Comforts

bain tourbillon	*baignoire à remous*	whirlpool bath
bain	*baignoire*	bathtub
balance	*pèse-personne*	scale
bol de toilette	*cuvette*	toilet bowl
chaîne	*chasse d'eau*	toilet flush
chambre de bain	*salle de bain*	bathroom
champlure	*robinet*	faucet
débarbouillette	*petite serviette de toilette*	washcloth

Tire la chaîne.
Actionne la chasse d'eau.
Flush the toilet.

La champlure coule.
Le robinet fuit.
The faucet is leaking.

On vient juss de s'faire poser un bain tourbillon.
*Nous venons tout juste de nous faire installer
une baignoire à remous.*
We just installed a whirlpool bath.

Creature Comforts

THE KITCHEN

canârd	*bouilloire*	kettle
chaudron	*casserole*	saucepan
dépense	*garde-manger*	food pantry/ cupboard
fourneau	*four*	oven
laveuse à vaisselle	*lave-vaisselle*	dishwasher
poêle	*cuisinière*	stove

On vous â mis un canârd su'l poêle.
Nous avons mis une bouilloire sur la cuisinière.
We put the kettle on the stove.

La laveuse à vaisselle se plogue après à' champlure.
Le lave-vaisselle se raccorde au robinet.
The dishwasher plugs into the faucet.

Allez-vous avwêr assez de chaudrons?
Allez-vous avoir suffisamment de casseroles?
Will you have enough saucepans?

Y'â de l'eau frwède dans le frigidaire.
Il y a de l'eau froide dans le réfrigérateur.
There is cold water in the refrigerator.

Creature Comforts

CLEANING UP

balayeuse	*aspirateur*	vacuum cleaner
boyau d'arrosage	*tuyau d'arrosage*	hose
chaudière	*seau*	bucket
époussetoir	*plumeau*	feather duster
frotter	*nettoyer*	to scrub
guénille	*torchon*	rag
laveuse	*lave-linge*	washing machine
minous	*moutons*	dust bunnies
porte-poussière	*pelle à poussière*	dustpan
sécheuse	*sèche-linge*	dryer
vadrouille	*balai à franges*	mop

Faudra bein que ch'pâsse la balayeuse.
Il faudrait bien que je passe l'aspirateur.
I really should vacuum.

Mets toute ton linge dans' laveuse. J'vâ m'en occuper.
Mets tous tes vêtements dans le lave-linge. Je vais m'en occuper.
Put your clothes in the washing machine. I'll take care of it.

Oublie pâs d'enlever é'minous avant d'partir la sécheuse.
N'oublie pas de nettoyer le filtre avant de faire démarrer le sèche-linge.
Don't forget to clean out the filter before you start the dryer.

Creature Comforts

62

Un p'tsi coup d'vadrouille vâ faire la djob.
Un simple coup de balai à franges fera l'affaire.
A little mopping will do the trick.

RESTAURANTS AND THE KITCHEN

bourré	*rassasié*	full
casse-croûte	*snack-bar*	snack bar
cuillère à table	*cuillère à soupe*	tablespoon
cuillère à thé	*cuillère à café*	teaspoon
déjeûner	*petit déjeûner*	breakfast
dîner	*déjeûner*	lunch
facture	*addition*	bill
souper	*dîner*	dinner/supper

Ch'peux-tsu vous apporter à' facture/le bill?
Puis-je vous apporter l'addition?
Should I bring you the bill?

On vâ t'êt bourré après çâ!
Nous allons être repus après avoir mangé tout cela.
We'll be full after this!

Creature Comforts

FOOD AND DRINK

beigne	*beignet*	donut
beurre de pinottes/d'arachides	*beurre de cacahuètes*	peanut butter
beurrée	*tartine*	slice of bread and butter
bière en fût	*bière pression*	draft beer/on tap
binnes	*fèves au lard*	baked beans
blé d'inde	*maïs*	corn on the cob
breuvage	*boisson*	beverage
broue	*mousse/bière*	froth/beer
chien chaud	*hot dog*	hot dog
crémage	*glaçage*	icing
liqueur	*boisson gazeuse*	soft drink
du manger	*de la nourriture*	food
melon d'eau	*pastèque*	watermelon
melon d'miel	*melon (chair vert clair)*	honeydew melon
motton	*grumeau*	lump
œufs au miroir	*œufs sur le plat*	fried egg (sunny side up)
pain doré	*pain perdu*	French toast

passé date
dont la date de fraîcheur est échue
past the best-before date

patate/pétaque	*pomme de terre*	potato
patates frites	*frites*	fries
patates pilées	*pommes de terre en purée*	mashed potatoes
piment/piment vert	*poivron*	pepper/ green pepper
poche de thé	*sachet de thé*	tea bag
préservatif	*agent de conservation*	preservative
roteux	*hot dog*	hot dog
rôties	*pain grillé*	toast
soda à pâte	*bicarbonate de soude*	baking soda
steak haché	*bœuf haché*	ground beef

Voulez-vous des rôties pour déjeûner?
Voulez-vous du pain grillé au petit déjeûner?
Would you like toast for breakfast?

se sucrer le bec
manger une sucrerie
to eat something sweet

saffe/cochon
gourmand/glouton
glutton

manger comme un cochon
manger beaucoup
to eat like a pig

se bourrer à' face/à' fraise
s'empiffrer
to stuff one's face

QUÉBÉCOIS CUISINE

BLEUET/BELUET/BELUA

The blueberry is very popular in the province of Québec and is usually associated with the region of Saguenay-Lac Saint-Jean. So much so, in fact, that the word **bleuet** itself has become a humorous reference to the inhabitants of this region. Wild blueberries are picked in late summer and are used in a wide array of pastries, pies and other sweet confections.

ATACÂ/ATOCÂ/CANNEBERGE

Cranberries are usually enjoyed in autumn, around Thanksgiving. Served as a sauce or jelly, they are savoured with turkey and game dishes. Cranberries are becoming increasingly popular in Québec due to their reputed health benefits.

CIPAILLE/SIPAILLE/CIPÂTE

Large meat pie containing potatoes and several kinds of meat, such as pork, beef, veal and even deer. Also called "**tourtière du Lac Saint-Jean.**"

ÉPLUCHETTE DE BLÉ D'INDE

This is basically a "corn on the cob" party. Around the month of August, people gather outdoors with friends and family and peel ears of corn by the sack load. The corn is then boiled in a large vat and enjoyed with salt and butter.

LES SUCRES/ALLER AUX SUCRES/ALLER À' CABANE À SUC'

"Sugaring off" or "going to the sugar shack" is a traditional springtime activity in Québec. Around this time, maple trees release their abundant sap, which is then collected and boiled. It is then transformed into **eau d'érable** (maple water), **sirop d'érable** (maple syrup) and **tire d'érable** (thick syrup or taffy that is poured over snow to harden and twisted around a stick, resulting in a maple lollipop.)

Going to the sugar shack is usually a joyous group event that includes a hearty, Québec-style meal. On the menu: regional delicacies such as ham, omelets, **fèves au lard** (baked beans and pork with maple syrup or molasses), **oreilles de crisse** (fried lard) and, of course, gallons of maple syrup.

You might also hear the expression **sirop de poteau** (literally "post syrup") in reference to maple syrup. This is a cheaper version of the real thing, usually mixed with other kinds of syrups or sugar and less expensive than pure syrup.

Creature Comforts

TIRE SAINTE-CATHERINE

This maple or molasses taffy is usually prepared in late September. Individually wrapped, the candy is then offered to children on Halloween (October 31) or Ste. Catherine's Day (November 25), which is basically "spinsters' day."

POUTINE

French fries covered with *fromage en grains* (cheese curds), which melt when heated. The concoction is then covered with brown gravy or tomato sauce (Italian poutine).

PÂTÉ CHINOIS

Shepherd's pie made with a bottom layer of ground beef, a middle layer of creamed corn and a top layer of mashed potatoes. The pie is then baked until the upper crust is golden.

SMOKED MEAT

For the best of this delicacy, Montréal is the place to be. Here, it is served on rye bread with a dill pickle.

CRETONS

This pâté of ground pork and lard is a traditional breakfast staple.

TOURTIÈRE

Meat pie (usually pork, beef and veal) that is prepared in various ways, according to family traditions. However, in the region of Saguenay-Lac Saint-Jean, the meat pie is known as *pâté à la viande,* since *tourtière* is something different: a large, deep-dish pie that consists of several kinds of meat, even game, and diced potatoes.

BÛCHE/BÛCHE DE NOËL

The "Christmas log" is a cake decorated with coloured icing, small trees and various "wintry" decorations.

POUDING-CHÔMEUR/POUDING AU CHÔMEUR

This dessert translates as "unemployment pudding" but is actually bread pudding. The recipe is quite simple: to a base of flour or soft bread pieces (without the crust), add oil, milk, eggs and maple syrup, then bake in the oven.

TARTE AU SUCRE

sugar pie

TARTE A' FARLOUCHE

This pie is made with molasses, flour and raisins.

Creature Comforts

GOING OUT

boucane	*fumée*	smoke
emboucaner	*enfumer*	to fill with smoke/ to smoke out
fin de semaine	*week-end*	weekend
plate	*ennuyeux*	boring
scinique	*montagnes russes*	roller-coaster
steppette	*pas de danse*	dance step
super le fonne	*vachement sympa*	lots of fun
toune	*air/mélodie/ chanson*	tune/melody/ song
vues	*cinéma*	cinema/movie

Tsu veux-tsu aller aux vues?
Veux-tu aller au cinéma?
Would you like to go the movies?

Y va y avwêr un méchant pârrté.
Il va y avoir toute une fête.
There's going to be a huge party./We'll have a blast.

On va avwêr un fonne nwêr.
Nous allons bien nous amuser.
We'll have a lot of fun.

Çé l'fonne à' mort!
C'est on ne peut plus amusant!/C'est très excitant!/C'est extrêmement divertissant!
This is so much fun!/This is very exciting!

Çé plate en bébitte./ Ça peut pâs êt' plus dolle.
Comme c'est ennuyeux./C'est triste à mourir.
This is so boring./That's very sad.

Tires-twé une bûche.
Assieds-toi./Va te chercher une chaise.
Have a seat./Get yourself a chair.

Y'â don bein d'la boucane icid'ans!
Ce qu'il peut y avoir de la fumée ici!
This place is so smoky!

Arrête de nous emboucaner avec ta cigarette.
Cesse de nous enfumer avec ta cigarette.
Stop smoking us out with your cigarette.

passer à' nuitte sa' corde à linge
passer une nuit blanche/veiller très tard
to spend a sleepless night/to stay up very late

Creature Comforts

se rincer le dalot/prendre un coup/
prendre un p'tit coup/
s'envoyer un verre en arrière d'la cravate/
se paqueter/s'pacter à' fraise/
e'rvirer une brosse/partir sa' brosse/
partir su' une baloune
prendre un (ou plusieurs) verre(s)
to have one (or several) drink(s)

caler une bière
boire une bière rapidement (ou d'un seul coup)
to down a beer

T'en bwé une shotte!
Tu bois beaucoup!
You sure drink a lot!

Y tinque en masse.
Il boit beaucoup.
He drinks a lot.

Ça donne un méchant bozz!
Ça étourdit!/Ça rend ivre!
That'll get you drunk!/That'll give you one heck of a buzz!

être éméché/être gorlot/être paqueté/
être saoul comme une botte
être ivre (à divers degrés)
To be drunk (to various degrees)

être faite/être faite à l'os
être complètement ivre
to be completely drunk

(Note that the expression *être faite/être faite à l'os* can also mean "to lose," "to know you're going to lose," "to be had," "to be going downhill," etc.)

SHOPPING

achalandé	*très fréquenté*	very busy
arranger	*réparer*	to fix
buanderie	*blanchisserie*	laundromat
centre d'achat	*centre commercial*	shopping mall
de seconde main	*usagé/d'occasion*	second-hand
dépanneur	*épicerie de dépannage*	convenience store
dî'ler	*marchander*	to haggle over ("to deal")
dispendieux	*cher/coûteux*	expensive
nettoyeur	*teinturier/pressing*	dry cleaner
neu	*neuf*	new
scrappe	*camelote*	junk ("scrap")
spécial/ vente	*solde*	on sale (reduced items)

Creature Comforts

TPS (taxe sur les produits et services)
taxe de vente fédérale
GST (Goods and Services Tax)

TVQ
taxe de vente du Québec
QST(Québec Sales Tax)

STATIONERY

aiguisoir	*taille-crayon*	pencil sharpener
attache-feuilles	*trombone*	paper clip
broche	*agrafe*	staple
brocheuse	*agrafeuse*	stapler
efface	*gomme à effacer*	eraser

HARDWARE

décapant	*dissolvant à vernis*	varnish/ paint remover
papier sâblé	*papier de verre/ d'émeri*	sandpaper

quincaillerie
quincaillerie/droguerie/marchand de couleurs
hardware store

sâbler	*poncer*	to sand
sâbleuse	*ponceuse*	sander
taraud	*écrou*	nut

GROOMING

fixatif/	*laque pour*	hair spray
spré nette ("Spray Net")	*les cheveux*	
poli à ongles	*vernis à ongles*	nail polish

MISCELLANEOUS ITEMS

carrosse	*landau/poussette*	stroller
enregistreuse	*magnétophone*	tape recorder
kodak	*appareil photo*	camera
pousse-pousse	*poussette*	stroller
ratine	*tissu-éponge*	terrycloth
système de son	*sono/chaîne stéréo*	stereo system

On peut vous l'arranger.
Nous pouvons vous le réparer.
We can fix it for you.

On n'â pâs de d'çâ.
Nous n'en avons pas.
We don't have any.

Y'ont rien qu'd'la scrappe, icitte.
Ils n'ont que de la camelote, ici.
All they have here is junk.

Y'â rien qu'du neu, icitte.
Il n'y a ici que du neuf.
Everything here is new.

On â réussi à y dî'ler çâ pâs cher.
Nous avons réussi à lui faire baisser son prix.
We managed to make him lower his price.

Ç't'un spécial que j'vous fais.
C'est un prix d'ami que je vous fais.
I'll give you a good deal.

Tout est en spécial.
Tout est en solde.
Everything is on sale.

Mont' don(c) wêr.
Montrez-le/-la, que je le/la voie.
Let me see that.

Combien vous voulez mette?
Combien êtes-vous disposé à payer?
How much are you willing to pay?

La taxe est pâs dans l'prix./Le prix comprend pâs é'taxes.
Le prix affiché n'inclut pas les taxes.
Taxes are not included in the price.

CLOTHING AND ACCESSORIES

bâs	*bas/chaussettes*	socks
bobettes	*petites culottes*	panties
bourse	*sac à main*	purse/handbag
cass/casque	*chapeau/casquette*	hat/cap
chandail	*chandail/t-shirt*	sweater/T-shirt

claques/chaloupes
caoutchoucs/couvre-chaussures
galoshes/rubber boots

cô'te (coat) d'habit	*veste*	suit jacket
costume de bain	*maillot de bain*	bathing suit
foulard	*écharpe*	scarf

gougounes
sandales de plage/pantoufles tricotés maison
flip-flops/homemade knit slippers

habit	*complet*	suit
jaquette	*chemise de nuit*	nightgown
kangourou	*sweat-shirt à poche centrale*	pocketed sweatshirt

Creature Comforts

mitaine	*moufle*	mitten
robe de chambre	*peignoir*	bathrobe
sacoche	*sac à main*	purse/handbag
tuque	*bonnet de laine*	wool hat
veste	*gilet/lainage*	cardigan
veston	*veste*	jacket

SPORTS

baloune	*ballon*	ball
ca'tcher	*attraper*	to catch
garnotter	*lancer avec force*	to throw with force
kicker	*botter*	to kick
scâ'rer	*marquer un but*	to score

Y'â ca'tché à' balle./Y'â ca'tché l'ballon.
Il a attrapé la balle/le ballon.
He caught the ball.

Y'â kické à' baloune.
Il a botté le ballon./Il a frappé le ballon du pied.
He kicked the ball.

Y t'y â enwèyé une méchante garnotte!
Il a frappé un de ces coups!
That was one heck of a throw!

Creature Comforts

78

HOCKEY

gô'ler	*garder les buts*	to be in goal/netminding
gô'lœrr	*gardien de but*	goalie

On va-tsu à' guêïme (game) de hockey?
Ça te dirait d'aller au match de hockey?
Do you want to go to the hockey game?

La Sainte Flanelle/Les Habitants
Le Canadien
The Canadiens/The Habs (Montréal's hockey team)

Les Canadiens jousent bein en maudzi.
Le Canadien joue vraiment très bien.
The Canadiens play very well.

Creature Comforts

HUMAN RELATIONS

GETTING INTIMATE

accoté	*en concubinage*	cohabitation
agace-pissette	*enjôleuse*	tease/ wily woman
bec	*bise/baiser* (noun)	kiss
blonde	*petite amie/ compagne*	girlfriend (romantic)
câsser	*rompre*	to break up
courâiller/ courir la galipote	*courir les jupons*	to be a woman-chaser
courâilleux	*coureur de jupons*	woman-chaser
domper	*laisser tomber*	to dump
fif/tapette/ moumoune (pej.)	*gay/gai*	gay man
fille de pârté	*fille qui aime faire la fête*	party girl
flocher	*laisser tomber*	to dump ("to flush")
gârs de pârté	*gars qui aime faire la fête*	party guy
guidoune/pute	*putain*	prostitute
jâser	*bavarder*	to chat
kick	*béguin*	crush (romantic)
krou'zer	*draguer*	to cruise

mettre/se mettre	*baiser* (verb)	to have sex
placoter	*bavarder*	to chat

pogner
avoir du succès/tripoter
to be (romantically) popular/to paw/to grab

prette	*prêt/prête*	ready
splitter	*rompre*	to break up
tchomme	*ami/petit ami/* *compagnon*	boyfriend

J'te présente mon tchomme.
Je te présente mon petit ami/mon compagnon.
I would like you to meet my boyfriend.

BUT (usually among people of the same gender)

Ç'te gârs-là, c'é mon meilleur tchomme.
Ce gars-là, c'est mon meilleur ami.
That guy's my best friend. ("chum")

OR

mé tchommes de filles
mes copines
my girlfriends

tomber en amour
tomber amoureux
to fall in love

À m'â donné un bec.
Elle m'a donné un baiser.
She gave me a kiss.

On â placoté une bonne demi-heure.
Nous avons bavardé pendant une bonne demi-heure.
We chatted for a good half-hour.

On a juss jâsé.
Nous avons simplement bavardé.
We just talked.

J'pense qu'à l'kick su mwé./J'pense qu'à l'â l'kick su mwé.
Je crois qu'elle a le béguin pour moi.
I think she has a crush on me.

Çé Paul qui nous â ma'tchés ensemble.
C'est Paul qui nous a présentés l'un à l'autre.
It was Paul who set us up.

À pogne pâs pantoute avec les gârs.
Elle n'a aucun succès auprès des garçons.
She has no success with boys.

BUT

Y m'â pogné é'fesses.
Il m'a tripoté les fesses.
He grabbed my buttocks.

Y sont accotés.
Ils vivent en concubinage.
They are living together (romantically).

J'te présente ma blonde.
Je te présente ma petite amie /ma compagne.
I would like you to meet my girlfriend (romantic).

Ça fa deux semaines qu'y'ont cassé/splitté.
Ça fait deux semaines qu'ils ont rompu.
They broke up two weeks ago.

Y l'â flochée./À'l l'â dompé.
Il/Elle l'a laissé tomber.
He/She dumped her/him.

Ch't'aime comme que t'é.
Je t'aime tel(le) que tu es.
I love you just the way you are.

Y pâsse son temps à courir la galipote.
C'est un coureur de jupons.
He's such a woman-chaser.

(On a "lighter" note, **courir la galipote** can also mean "going out"
or "gallivanting," as in **T'es encore allé courir la galipote?**)

HUMAN RELATIONS

accommoder	*rendre service*	to do someone a favour
achaler	*importuner*	to bother someone
batâille	*se battre*	fight (physical)
binne/bette	*visage (expression)*	facial expression
bitcher	*critiquer*	to complain ("to bitch")
bretter	*lambiner*	to dawdle
ca'tcher	*comprendre*	to understand ("to catch")
chicane	*dispute*	argument/ quarrel
djôker	*faire des blagues*	to joke around
enfarger	*faire trébucher*	to trip someone up
enfirwâper	*embrouiller (quelqu'un)*	to confuse someone
ertontir	*arriver à l'improviste*	to arrive unexpectedly
ervenger	*venger*	to avenge
menterie	*mensonge*	lie
niaisage	*badinage/ temps perdu en futilités*	fooling around/ wasting time frivolously

Human Relations

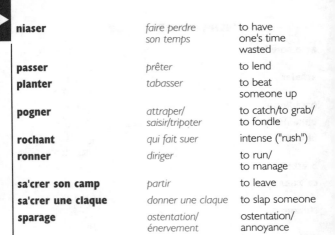

niaser	*faire perdre son temps*	to have one's time wasted
passer	*prêter*	to lend
planter	*tabasser*	to beat someone up
pogner	*attraper/ saisir/tripoter*	to catch/to grab/ to fondle
rochant	*qui fait suer*	intense ("rush")
ronner	*diriger*	to run/ to manage
sa'crer son camp	*partir*	to leave
sa'crer une claque	*donner une claque*	to slap someone
sparage	*ostentation/ énervement*	ostentation/ annoyance
troster	*faire confiance*	to trust

zigonner
tourner en rond/s'acharner sans succès/perdre son temps en futilités
to go round in circles/to struggle unsuccessfully/to waste one's time frivolously

Tsu y'â tsu vu a'binne/bette?
As-tu remarqué son expression?/Quelle tête il fait!
Did you see his face?/What a face she's making!

Si ça peut vous accommoder…
Si ça vous arrange…/Si ça peut vous rendre service…
If that'll help you out…

Human Relations

Tsu parles d'un nom à coucher dwâor!
Quel nom bizarre!
What a strange name!

Tasse-twé!/Tasse-twé d'lâ!/Tasse-twé de d'lâ!
Pousse-toi!/Dégage!/Fais de l'air!
Move!/Get out of here!/Get out of the way!

Wôwe les moteurs!
On se calme!
Calm down!

Les nerfs!
Ne t'énerve pas comme ça!
Take it easy!/Cool your jets!

Tsu m'passes-tsu ton livre?
Me prêtes-tu ton livre?
Will you lend me your book?

Awèye!/Embrèye!/Dziguédzine!
Dépêche-toi!/Cesse de lambiner!/Accélère!
Hurry up!/Let's go!/Step on it!

Achale-mwé pâs.
Laisse-moi tranquille./Cesse de m'importuner.
Leave me alone./Stop bothering me.

Arrête don(c)!

Tu n'es pas sérieux?/C'est une blague?/Tu veux rire ?/J'ai du mal à te croire.

Are you serious?/Is this a joke?/Are you joking?/I don't believe it.

Arrête don(c) d'bitcher cont' toute!

Cesse donc de tout critiquer!

Stop complaining about everything!

Arrête tes sparages!

Cesse de t'énerver pour rien!/Cesse de gesticuler!/Cesse de nous en mettre plein la vue!

Don't get excited for nothing!/Stop gesticulating!/Stop showing off!

Arrête de twister tout ce que ch'te dzi.

Cesse de déformer tout ce que je te dis.

Stop twisting my words around.

Arrête don(c) de bretter!

Cesse donc de lambiner!

Stop dawdling!

Arrête don(c) de zigonner!

Cesse donc de jouer avec cela!/
N'as-tu pas fini de perdre ton temps?/
Arrête de tourner autour du pot!
Stop playing around!/
Will you stop wasting your time?/
Get to the point!

Arrête don(c) de niaiser!

Cesse donc de dire des bêtises!/Cesse donc de faire le pitre!/Cesse
donc de te moquer!/Cesse donc de perdre ton temps en futilités!
Stop talking nonsense!/Stop fooling around!/Stop acting like an
idiot!/Stop wasting your time!

J'aime pâs çâ m'faire niaiser.

Je n'aime pas qu'on se paie ma tête.
I don't like being ridiculed.

Si y pouvait arrêter d'niaiser, ça irait pâs mal plus vite.

S'il ne lambinait pas tant, ça irait beaucoup plus vite.
If only he could stop dawdling, it would go much faster.

J'ca'tche pâs ton affaire.

Je ne comprends rien à ce que tu dis/à ce que tu fais.
I don't understand what you're talking about/what you're doing.

Human Relations

parler dans l'casse/casque
dire ses quatre vérités à quelqu'un/engueuler
to tell someone the plain truth/to yell at someone

Y t'y â parlé su' un vrai temps.
Il lui a parlé sans ménager ses paroles.
He spoke to him quite harshly.

pogner une chicane
avoir une dispute
to have an argument/a quarrel

J'l'ai pogné juss à temps.
Je l'ai attrapé juste à temps.
I caught him just in time.

Ch'te dzi qu'à s'é faite planter!
Elle s'est fait solidement tabasser.
She got seriously beaten up./She got beat hands down.

passer au cash/manger une claque/
manger une volée/manger toute une volée
se faire tabasser
to get roughed up/beaten up

Ça' pâs pris d'temps qu'à s'é 'rvengée.
Elle n'a guère mis de temps à se venger.
She wasted no time getting her revenge.

brâsser le cadran
secouer vivement
to shake (someone) up

Nos voisins sont pâs mal rochants.
Nos voisins nous font passablement suer.
Our neighbours are a pain in the neck.

Cé rochant, c't'affaire-lâ!
Ce n'est pas de tout repos, cette histoire-là!
This situation is no picnic!

Tchèke-twé bein!
Fais bien attention à toi!
Take good care of yourself!

Ça' pâs rapport!
Ça n'a aucun rapport!
That has nothing to do with it!

BUT

Y'â pâs rapport./Y'â pâs rap'.

*Il est complètement dans l'erreur./Il est complètement déphasé./
Il divague./Il n'a rien à faire ici.*
He's completely mistaken./He is so not with it./
He's rambling./He doesn't belong here.

Human Relations

Vâs-y fort!
Ne te gêne surtout pas!
Feel free!/Go right ahead!

Y'arrête pas d'ronner tout le monde!
Il ne cesse de donner des ordres à tout le monde!
He keeps bossing people around!

WORKING

barbier	*coiffeur pour hommes*	barber
briqueleur	*briqueteur/maçon*	brick-layer
châroèyer	*transporter*	to carry
clairer	*renvoyer/ éliminer*	to fire/ to eliminate ("to clear")
comptable-agréé (CA)	*expert-comptable*	chartered accountant
dactylo	*machine à écrire*	typewriter
en charge	*responsable*	in charge
flopper	*rater*	to miss ("to flop")

gô'ler
se dépêcher/s'activer
to hurry up/to get busy ("to goal")

kicker dwâor
mettre à la porte avec fracas
to fire ("to kick")

opérer
fonctionner/agir
to function/to act

patenteux
bricoleur ingénieux
do-it-yourselfer

pédaler
aller vite/être rapide
to go fast/to be quick

pogner
accrocher/avoir du succès
to catch/to be successful

rodé
entraîné/préparé/pleinement fonctionnel
trained/prepared/fully functional

ronner
diriger
to run

sarrau
blouse (de laboratoire/de médecin, etc.)
lab coat

surtemps
heures supplémentaires
overtime

toffer
durer/persister/tenir
to last/to persist/to hold ("tough"/"tough" it out)

vidangeur
éboueur
garbage collector

À l'â complètement floppé son examen.
Elle a complètement raté son examen.
She failed her exam.

s'enfarger din fleurs du tapis
se mettre les pieds dans les plats/se perdre en détails confus et inutiles
to put one's foot in it/to waste time on unnecessary details

Human Relations

Y'ont pas toffé deux mois.
Ils n'ont pas tenu deux mois.
They didn't last two months.

J'me su faite clairer.
J'ai été remercié/renvoyé.
I was fired.

J'ai réussi à clairer toutes mes dettes.
J'ai réussi à liquider toutes mes dettes.
I finally paid off my debts.

Çé lui qui ronne la place.
C'est lui qui dirige, ici.
He's the one who runs the place.

THE FAMILY

flo	*enfant*	child
fille	*fille*	daughter
gârs	*fils*	son
matante Hélène	*tante Hélène*	Aunt Hélène
môman	*maman*	mom
mononcle Roger	*oncle Roger*	Uncle Roger
pôpa	*papa*	dad
trâlée	*bande/ribambelle*	group/swarm

Human Relations

Comment vont tes flos?
Comment vont tes enfants?
How are your kids?

Ch't'allé chez mon mononc' pi ma matante.
Je suis allé chez mon oncle et ma tante.
I visited my uncle and aunt.

Y t'ont une méchante trâlée d'enfants.
Ils ont vraiment beaucoup d'enfants.
They have a lot of kids. (Note that **trâlée** can also be used to designate any group of people or things.)

FEELINGS

avwêr des bébittes
être quelque peu névrosé/avoir des problèmes personnels
to be somewhat neurotic/to have personal problems

avwêr la chienne
avoir peur/ne pas avoir le cran de faire quelque chose
to be afraid/to lack the guts to do something

BUT

avwêr l'air d'la chienne à Jâcques
être mal habillé/coiffé/maquillé/avoir l'air fatigué/abattu/déprimé
to be badly dressed/coiffed/made up/to look tired/worn out/depressed

avwêr d'la misère
en arracher
to have a hard time

avwêr d'la misère à toffer à'ronne
avoir du mal à tenir le coup
to have a hard time holding up

avwêr le motton
être triste/avoir la gorgé serrée
to be sad/to have a lump in one's throat

avwêr son troc/son voyage/en avwêr plein l'cass
en avoir assez/par-dessus la tête
to have enough

capoter/capoter bein raide
s'énerver/paniquer/perdre la tête
to get worked up/to panic/to lose one's head

être tout à l'envers
être complètement retourné/bouleversé
to be distressed

être débiné/pâs mal débiné
être plus ou moins décontenancé
to be disconcerted

être désappointé/pâs mal désappointé
être plus ou moins déçu
to be disappointed

être flagadou
être raplapla
to be washed out

être sa' bomme/pâs mal sa' bomme
être plus ou moins fatigué
to be tired/bummed out

tripper
s'amuser
to have fun ("to trip")

Ça trippe-tsu?
On s'amuse?
Are we having fun?

Ça trippe fort!
On s'amuse follement!
We're having a blast!

badtripper
paniquer/souffrir/être dans tous ses états
to panic/to suffer/to be in a bad state ("bad trip")

être tanné/pâs mal tanné/tanné au boutte
fatigué/las/désabusé/déprimé/incapable de supporter plus longtemps
to be tired/weary/disillusioned/depressed/unable to stand it any longer

faire la baboune
bouder
to sulk

faire le saut/djom'per/stepper
sursauter
to be startled ("jump"/"step")

filer doux
se montrer aussi docile et discret que possible
to be docile and discreet

filer un mauvais coton
traverser une mauvaise passe/
ne pas se sentir bien/être de mauvaise humeur
to go through bad times/to feel bad/
to be in a bad mood

avwêr le caquet bâs
avoir la mine basse
to pull a long face

Human Relations

manger ses bâs
ronger son frein/être mal à l'aise/regretter amèrement/
être dans tous ses états
to chomp at the bit/to feel ill at ease/to regret/
to be in a bad state

J'en peux pu.
Je n'en peux plus.
I can't take it anymore.

rocher
éprouver des difficultés/passer un mauvais moment
to have difficulty/to have a hard time

virer su'l top
perdre la tête
to lose one's head

BEHAVIOURS AND ATTITUDES

accoté
accoudé/appuyé
to lean on/against

baveux
taquin/méprisable
a teasing/contemptible person

Human Relations

bla'ster	*engueuler*	to yell at ("to blast")
capoté	*original/ fantasiste/ téméraire*	original/ eccentric/ reckless
croche	*malhonnête*	dishonest
feluette	*gringalet*	puny
fin/fine	*gentil/gentille*	kind/nice
gougoune	*niais/idiot*	simpleton/idiot
grand djack	*homme de grande taille*	tall man ("Jack")
naiseux/nono/ toton/épais	*imbécile/ abruti/niais*	imbecile/ moron/idiot

ostineux
qui aime à s'obstiner/contredire/disputer
stubborn/argumentative

pèté/sauté/flyé
original/fantaisiste/excentrique/téméraire
original/eccentric/reckless

pèteux de broue	*prétentieux*	pretentious
pissou	*peureux/ soupe au lait*	scaredy-cat

poche
malhabile/peu doué/mauvais/faible
clumsy/not bright/bad/poor/(Although this term is pronounced like the English word "posh," the two words have completely opposite meanings.)

quétaine	*ringuard*	corny/tacky
ratoureux	*joueur de tour*	trickster
robineux	*clochard*	homeless person
sans-dessein	*imbécile/ idiot/stupide*	imbecile/ idiot/stupid
slô'mô	*lent/au relenti*	slow ("slow motion")
smatte	*gentil/habile/ intelligent*	smart/kind/clever
snô'rô	*coquin*	rascal
stické	*accroché*	stuck
Ti-djo connaissant	*Monsieur sait-tout*	Mr. Know-It-All
tocson	*rustre/costaud*	boor/strong
twister	*déformer*	to twist
vlimeux/vlimeuse	*espiègle*	mischievous

Y'était accoté sa' tab.
Il était accoudé sur la table.
His elbows were on the table.

Accote-twé pâs su'l mur.
Ne t'appuie pas contre le mur.
Don't lean against the wall.

avwêr du front (tout l'tour d'la tête)
*avoir du cran (à revendre)/ne pas avoir froid aux yeux/être
malpoli/impertinent/audacieux*
to have a lot of nerve/to be impolite/impertinent/bold

È pâs bein fine avec lui.
Elle n'est pas très gentille avec lui.
She's not very nice to him.

T'é don(c) bein gougoune!
Ce que tu peux être idiot!
You're such an idiot!

BUT

Tsu m'as d'l'air pâs mal gougoune!
Tu me sembles être plutôt dans les vapes!
You seem to have your head in the clouds!

un espèce de grand jack
quelqu'un de particulièrement grand (et généralement mince)
a particularly tall (and usually thin) man

Tsu parles d'un sans-dessein!
Quel imbécile!
What an imbecile!

Human Relations

Comment s'qu'y'é (est-ce qu'il est) t'amanché?
Comment peut-il être aussi mal habillé?
What a terrible outfit he's wearing!

T'é bein baveux!
Ce que tu peux être taquin/provocateur!
You're such a rascal/an agitator!

Çé rien qu'un maudzi baveux!
C'est un personnage méprisable/exécrable au plus point.
He's a despicable/atrocious person.

Y te l'â blasté d'aplomb!
Il l'a sérieusement engueulé!
He really gave him hell/blasted him.

Y s'é faite blaster pâs rien qu'à peu près!
Il s'est fait engueuler comme pas deux.
He really got yelled at/blasted.

Ç't'un gârs croche.
C'est quelqu'un de malhonnête.
He's a dishonest man.

BUT

Y'â é' zyeux croches.
Il louche.
He's cross-eyed.

Y'arrêtent pâs d's'ostiner, ces deux-là.

Ils n'arrêtent pas de se disputer/de se tenir tête, ces deux-là.

Those two can't stop arguing.

Ç'te fille-là, è complètement pètée/sautée/flyée.

Cette fille-là est vraiment excentrique./Cette fille-là n'a aucune limite.

That girl is really eccentric/out there.

T'é rien qu'un pèteux de broue!

Ce que tu peux être prétentieux.

You are so pretentious!

T'é bein poche!

Ce que tu peux être maladroit/malhabile!/Ce que tu peux mal jouer!/Tu n'es vraiment pas doué!

You're so clumsy/useless!/You're such a bad player!/You have no talent whatsoever!

BUT

Ça vaut pâs cher la poche.

Ça n'a vraiment que très peu de valeur.

It's not really worth much.

T'é don(c) bein ratoureux!

Ce que tu peux aimer jouer des tours!/Tu te paies vraiment la tête des gens!/Tu nous as encore eus!

You really like to play tricks on others, don't you?/You got us again!

Human Relations

Y'é slô'mô comme ça s'peut pas!

Il est on ne peut plus lent!

He is so slow/dim-witted!

Y'é pâs mal smatte.

Il est plutôt gentil et serviable./Il est passablement habile de ses mains./Il fait preuve d'une certaine intelligence.

He's somewhat friendly./He can be handy./He's pretty smart.

BUT

Fa pâs ton smatte.

Ne te montre pas plus intelligent que tu ne l'es./N'essaie pas de nous impressionner.

Don't act smarter than you are./Don't try to impress us./Don't be a smart-ass or smart-alec.

Ç't'un méchant gorlot.

Il n'a vraiment aucun jugement.

He lacks good judgment.

Ch'te trouve pâs mal hèvé.

Je te trouve très dur./
Je trouve que tu insistes très lourdement./
Il me semble que tu t'imposes pas mal.

I find you quite heavy/pushy./
I think you're insisting too much./
You seem to be imposing yourself.

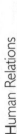

Human Relations

Tsu parles d'un drôle de moineau!

Tu parles d'un original!/
Quel personnage fantaisiste/farfelu/bizarre/étrange!

What an eccentric!/
What a crazy/strange character!

Twé, mon snô'rô!

Coquin, va!

You little rascal!

Y'é stické su son idée.

Il ne démord pas de son idée.

He's sticking to his idea.

Ch'te trouve pâs mal tchî'pe.

Je te trouve bien mesquin.

I find you quite stingy ("cheap").

È bein strêït avec tout le monde.

Elle se montre toujours droite, juste et intègre avec tous.

She's always fair ("straight") with everyone.

BUT

Ça s'peut pâs comment ç'qu'è strêït!

Elle est tellement stricte et rigide!

She's so strict and inflexible!

Human Relations

Un vra ti-djo connaissant!
Il a toujours réponse à tout, celui-là!
He's such a know-it-all!

Ça s'peut-tsu êt' twitte de même!
Comment peut-on être aussi stupide/simple d'esprit!
How can anyone be so stupid/dim-witted/such a "twit"?

Y leur a twisté ça...
Il leur a raconté n'importe quoi.
He completely distorted/"twisted" the truth.

Àn' n'a d'dans!/Y n'a d'dans!
Elle a de l'énergie à revendre!/Il a de l'énergie à revendre!
She's got energy to spare!/He's got energy to spare!

être din patates/din choux/dans le champ
être dans l'erreur/à côté de ses pompes
to be full of it/to be completely mistaken

être magané/poqué
être fatigué/affaibli/amoché/en piteux état
to be tired/weak/to look a mess/to be in a sorry state

se faire maganer
se faire maltraiter/malmener
to be mistreated/abused

Y'é tsu quétaine, yeinqu'ein peu!
Ce qu'il peut être ringard!
He is so tacky!
Note that *quétaine* is also commonly used to designate any tacky or corny thing or situation.

Human Relations

OTHER WORDS AND EXPRESSIONS

MORE QUÉBÉCOIS

au plus sacrant	*au plus vite*	as soon as possible
brun	*marron*	brown
écartillé	*écarté/écartelé*	spread apart
garrocher	*lancer*	to throw
gorgoton	*gorge*	throat
oubedon	*ou*	or
paqueter	*empaqueter/ faire ses bagages*	to pack
spotter	*repérer*	to spot
supposé	*censé*	supposed
supposément	*censément*	supposedly
tataouinage	*complication inutile*	needless complication

tataouiner/taponner/zigonner
perdre (ou faire perdre) son temps/manipuler distraitement/tourner en rond/badiner
wasting time/doing something distractedly/fooling around

ambitionner
exagérer
to exaggerate

Ayoye!
Ça fait mal!/Quelle déclaration percutante!
Ouch!

bécosses
W.C.
washroom

gosser
travailler le bois au couteau
to whittle a piece of wood

BUT

This term can also mean "to beat around the bush," "to struggle without success," "to return to the attack" or "to waste one's time."

venir
Sometimes replaces *devenir* ("to become");
can also mean "to reach orgasm."

Ça y vâ en grand/en grande!/Ça y vâ par là!
On fait les choses en grande!/Ça va vite!
To do something in a big way./That's quick!

Cé tsiguidou./Toute é tsiguidou.
Ça va très bien./Tout est parfait.
Fine.

Ç'pâs des farces.
On ne rigole plus.
Seriously./It's not a joke.

Ç'pâs l'yâb (le diable).
Ça ne vaut pas grand-chose.
It's not worth much.

Ç'pâs l'yâb mieux.
Ce n'est guère mieux.
That's not much better.

Le yâb é pogné dans' cabane./La chicane é pognée.
On s'engueule ferme là-dedans./Les hostilités sont ouvertes./Ils ont une dispute.
There's a lot of fighting in there./They are fighting.

Ç'pâs coulé dans l'béton, leur affaire.
Rien n'est moins sûr./Tout peut encore changer./Ils n'ont peut-être pas tout à fait raison.
Nothing is certain/set in stone./They might be wrong.

Ça vâ mal à' shoppe.
Ça va mal./Ça ne se passe pas comme prévu.
Things are not going well/as planned.

Other Words and Expressions

Ch't'en pâsse un papier!
Tu l'as dit!/On ne rigole plus!
You said it!/No joke!

ch'ter (jeter) **ses choux grâs**	*gaspiller*	to waste
débouler	*dévaler/dégringoler*	to tumble down

Y t'leur â déboulé çâ!
Il leur a dit tout ce qu'il avait sur le cœur./Il leur a déballé son sac./Il leur a débité l'information en un rien de temps.
He told them what was on his mind./He poured his heart out./He gave them the information in mere seconds.

en tsitsi	*beaucoup*	a lot
en r'venir	*s'en remettre*	to get over it

États-Unis
In reference to the United States, you will often hear **lé zétâs**, **lé s'tâ zunis**, **aux zétâs** and even **aux Stêïtss** (States).

prendre une débarque/pogner une méchante débarque
trébucher/échouer
to trip/to fall down/to fail

sur un vrai temps
tout à fait/à fond
quite/entirely/thoroughly

Other Words and Expressions

114

Ça y vâ sur un vrai temps!
Ça roule à pleine vapeur!
It's going at full speed!

Y'en â en masse./Y'en â pour les fins p'é fous./Y'en â un châr pi une barge.
Il y en a amplement/énormément/plus qu'il n'en faut.
There's plenty/more than enough.

Ça r'garde mal.
Ce s'annonce mal./C'est de mauvaise augure./C'est un mauvais signe.
It's not looking good./It's a bad sign.

Y'â 'rvolé à terre.
Il a été projeté par terre.
He was thrown to the ground.

Le sang 'rvolait partout.
Le sang pissait dans tous les sens.
Blood was gushing out everywhere.

Quant à l'â échappé son verre, ça 'rvolé su mwé.
Quant elle a laissé tomber son verre, son contenu m'a éclaboussé.
When she dropped her glass, it splashed all over me.

Quand la vit' â pèté, ch'te dzi (je te dis) qu'ça 'rvolé!
Quand la vitre s'est brisée, elle a volé en éclats!
When the window was broken, it smashed into pieces!

Other Words and Expressions

Mets-en, ç'pâs d'l'onguent!
Ne te gêne surtout pas pour en mettre!/Sers-moi généreusement./Appliques-en une bonne couche!
Don't be shy; pile it on!/Give me a hearty portion./Apply generously!

Yeinqu'à wêr (voir), on wé (voit) bein!
Il suffit de regarder pour se rendre à l'évidence./C'est l'évidence même!/Comment peut-on être assez bête pour be pas voir ce qu'il en est vraiment?
Just look and see./It's so obvious!/How can you not see what's going on?

un m'man' n'é
à un moment donné/en temps et lieu
one of these days/in due course

Bein wèyons (voyons) don(c)!
N'exagère tout de même pas!/Soyons sérieux!/Cela n'a aucun sens!
Don't exaggerate!/Let's be serious./That makes no sense!

Y'â toujours bein un boutte!
Il y a tout de même des limites!
There's a limit to everything!

Woup' élaï!
Oops!
Oops!

CURSING

By no means is this section intended to encourage you to use the words and expressions described. On the contrary, we strongly recommend you avoid going down that treacherous road, for not only will you probably have a hard time pronouncing them correctly and in the proper context, but you might also upset or offend others.

The reason we are incorporating this section on cursing is merely to help you recognize these expressions from the mouths of locals, since they are still quite frequent in Québécois French. Although some of these words and expressions are commonplace, they are still vulgar.

In this section you will notice a wide array of references to religion and sacred objects (**sacrer** actually means "to swear" or, more precisely, "to vulgarize sacred words"). Indeed, the Catholic religion played a pivotal role in Québec until the 1960s, and the clergy had a very strong influence on all spheres of society. Eventually, the people revolted against the abuses of the Church by removing the sacred aspect of the holy objects that symbolized it.

Bâtârd!
Bastard

Baptême!
Baptism. Toned-down versions of this term are **batèche** and **batêche**.

Câliss!
Chalice. Toned-down versions of this term are **câlik**, **câline** and **câline de binne**.

câlisser son camp
to leave

câlisser une volée
to hit someone

Calvaire!
Calvary. Toned-down versions of this term are **calvette**, **calvinus** and even **joualvert**, which could also mean **cheval vert** ("green horse").

Ciboire!/Cibwêre!
Ciborium. The toned-down version of this term is **câlibwêre**, a combination of **câliss** and **cibwêre**. This word can also be preceded by "**saint**": être en saint cibwère.

Criss!
Christ. Toned-down versions of this term are **cliss** and **crime**.

crisser un coup de poing
to punch someone

décrisser
to leave in a hurry

This term, as well as **dékâlisser** and **déconcrisser**, can mean "to destroy," "to demolish" or "to break," as in **Mon châr est toute dékâlissé/décrissé/déconcrissé**. The same words can also mean "to be depressed" or "to be bent out of shape," as in **Chu toute dékâlissé/décrissé d'la vie**.

foqué
crazy/unhinged ("fucked")

Maudzi!
Damned or cursed. Toned-down versions of this term are **maudzine** and **saudzi**.

Ostie/Stie!
Host (bread consecrated in the Eucharist). Toned-down versions of this term are **esti** and **ostinâtion**.

Other Words and Expressions

Sacrament!
Means the same in both languages. This word can also be preceded by "**saint**": **être en saint sacrament**.

Simonac!
This word can also be preceded by "**saint**": **être en saint simonac.**

Tabarnak/Tabernacle!
Means the same in both languages. Toned-down versions of this curse are **tabarnanne**, **tabarslak**, **tabarnouche** and **tabarouette**.

Târieu!
Bastard or bitch, as in **le târieu** or **la târieuse**.

Être en baptême, en calvaire, en criss, en tabarnak, en bâtârd, en beau joualvert, en beau maudzi, en saint sacrament, en târieu, etc.
to be furious

Note that all of these curse words can be used for emphasis without denoting anger or negation (but without lessening their vulgarity): **d'la maudzite bonne bouffe** ("really good food"), **une criss de belle fille** ("a really good-looking girl"), **un esti d'bon gârs** ("a really nice guy"), **un ostie d'grosse côte** ("a really steep hill").

And of course, let's not forget that one foul substance that translates into all languages…

Merde!/D'la marde!
Shit!

Maudzite marde!
What a shame!/What a bummer!

T'é plein d'marde!
You're full of it!

T'é don(c) bein mardeux!
You are so lucky!

Çé juss d'la marde!
It's pure luck.

Ça vaut pâs d'la marde.
It's not worth much.

Chu dans marde jusqu'au cou.
I'm swimming in it.

Mange d'la marde!
Eat shit!/Go to hell!

Other Words and Expressions

Çé l'boutte d'la marde!
Now I've seen it all!

Thankfully, **marde** is often toned down to **chnoutte**.

UNKNOWN WORDS

The following words are common in European French but are unknown by the vast majority of French Canadians. Here are their equivalents to make sure that you are well understood (the European term is first, followed by the Québécois term and the English translation).

blatte/cafard	**coquerelle**	cockroach
blanchisserie	**buanderie**	laundromat
caddie	**poussette**	stroller
chouchou	**élastique pour les cheveux**	hair elastic
droguerie	**quincaillerie**	hardware store
gendarmerie	**poste de police**	police station
laque	**fixatif**	hairspray
P.-V. (procès-verbal)	**contravention**	fine/ticket
pain perdu	**pain doré**	French toast
pastèque	**melon d'eau**	watermelon
PCV	**frais virés**	collect call
poncer	**sâbler**	to sand
potiron	**citrouille**	pumpkin

Other Words and Expressions

122

préservatif	**condom**	condom
pressing/teinturier	**nettoyeur**	dry cleaner
PTT	**bureau de poste**	post office
rutabaga	**navet**	turnip/rutabaga
serpillière	**moppe**	mop
shamalo	**guimauve**	marshmallow
socquettes	**petits bas courts**	ankle socks
sopalin	**essuie-tout**	paper towel
sparadrap	**plaster/ diachylon**	adhesive bandage
TTC	**taxes incluses**	tax included

You should also note that if you use the word *fermer* to indicate "to lock" (as you would in Europe), you may get a nasty surprise. Indeed, in Québec, **fermer** only means "to close," so if you want a door to be locked, make sure you say **vérouiller** or **barrer**.

THOSE DECEPTIVE FAUX AMIS

Finally, it is important to know that some words that are used as much in French Canada as in Europe have completely different meanings.

abreuvoir
This is not for animals, as in Europe, but rather a water fountain for humans.

achalandé
Here, this word means "very busy" and refers to a shop. In Europe, it means "well-stocked."

adonner
Instead of "devoting oneself to something," as in Europe, this translates as "great timing," as in **ça adonne bein**, or "convenient," as in **ça t'adonnes-tsu d'y aller aujourd'hui?**

affaire
Here, this refers to an undefined thing, as in **cé quoi ç't'affaire-là?**, or situation, **as in tsu parles din n'affaire!** Here are other examples:

V'lâ (voilà) une bonne affaire de faite!
It's a good thing that's done.

Ç'pâs d'tes affaires.
That's none of your business.

Y'ont pâs d'affaire lâ.
They have no business there./They shouldn't be there.

Ç't'ein n'affaire de rien.
It's nothing./No trouble.

Pâs d'affaire!
No way!

allure
You may recognize certain standard expressions such as **avoir fière allure** or **filer à toute allure**, but here are two more that are typical of Québécois French:

À' pas d'allure.
She lacks judgment./She has no manners.

Ça' pâs d'allure.
That makes no sense.

bâs
In Europe, this only means "stockings," but here, the term also means "socks."

bloc
In addition to the usual definitions and expressions associated with this word:

avoir un mal de bloc
to have a headache

faire le tour du bloc
to walk around the block

bord
In addition to the usual definitions and expressions
associated with this word:

d'l'aut' bord d'la table
on the opposite side of the table

Êtes-vous d'mon bord?
Are you on my side?

Chu su'l bord d'arriver.
I'm almost there.

prendre le bord
to leave in a hurry

caler
In Québécois French, this word can mean several things:

caler dans' neige/dans' bwette
to sink in snow/in mud

caler quelqu'un
to belittle someone

Other Words and Expressions

Y cale autant que son père.
He's losing his hair as much as his father.

caler une bière
to down a beer

chaudière
In Europe, this means "boiler"; in Québec, it translates as "bucket."

claque
In addition to meaning "slap in the face," Québécois speakers use this term to mean "to give it all you've got," **as in donnes-y à' claque.**

Also, if a salesperson offers you a pair of **claques**, don't whip out your boxing gloves; he or she is simply referring to galoshes (rubber over boots or wellies).

couvert/couverte
Here, the first means "lid," while the second, which can also be pronounced **couvarte**, means "blanket."

d'abord
This expression loosely translates as "then" or "if that's the way it is": **j'irai pâs, d'abord**.

Other Words and Expressions

débarquer
In addition to the usual definitions and expressions associated with this word:

débarquer de l'autobus/de la chaise
to get off the bus/the chair

Sa chaîne de bécyk â débarqué.
His bicycle chain fell off.

débarquer d'une équipe
to quit a team

déjeuner/dîner/souper
Don't forget that, unlike in Europe, these are respectively breakfast, lunch and dinner/supper.

écarter
Who would have guessed that this word, which usually means "to spread," could also mean "to lose"?

J'ai écarté ma mont'.
I lost my watch.

On s'é t'écartés.
We got lost.

È pâs mal écartée.
She's rather lost/confused.

échapper
In Québécois French, this means "to drop," as in **j'ai échappé mon couteau.**

écœurant
This term, which usually means "disgusting," can take on the opposite meaning in Québécois French: "fabulous," "extraordinary," "great," etc.

embarquer
In addition to the usual definitions and expressions associated with this word:

embarquer dans l'autobus/sur une chaise
to get on the bus/to climb onto a chair

embarquer dans' police/dans une équipe
to join the police force/a team

J'y'en ai parlé, mais y'embarque pâs pantoute.
I told him about it, but he's not enthusiastic at all.

guénille
This word has two additional meanings here:

Other Words and Expressions

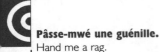

Pâsse-mwé une guénille.
Hand me a rag.

À travaille dans guénille.
She works in the clothing industry/rag trade.

gosses
In Québécois, this term does not designate children but rather testicles, so avoid sentences such as **embrasse tes gosses pour moi!**

marquer
In addition to the usual definitions and expressions associated with this word:

Dans sa let', à' pâs marqué où est-ce qu'ê'tait.
In her letter, she didn't mention where she was.

As-tsu marqué ton nom sa' liss?
Did you put your name on the list?

J'm'en souviens pu, j'l'ai pâs marqué.
I don't remember, I didn't write it down.

masse
This word means "very," as in **ça glisse en masse**, and "enough," as in **on â en masse de monde.**

misère

The expression **avoir d'la misère** is translated as "to have difficulty."

par exemple

In addition to its usual meaning ("for example"), this expression often replaces par contre ("however"), as in **j'va t'dzire quelque chose, mais j'veux pâs qu'tsu l'répètes, par exemple.**

passer

Pâsse-moi un 20 may sound a lot like **passe-moi le sel**, but note that if you agree to this request, it might be a while before you see that $20 bill again. Indeed, in this context, passer means "to lend."

pèter

Aside from the colourful meaning we all know, here are some more:

être pèté

to be eccentric

Vâ don(c) pèter din fleurs!

Get lost!

On â complètement pèté l'budget.

We went over budget.

Other Words and Expressions

pèter plus haut que l'trou/n'être qu'un pèteux de broue
to be pretentious

se pèter à' margoulette
to fall flat on one's face

piler
In Québec, this word takes on the unusual meaning of "to walk on," as in **pile pâs su'l gâzon.**

piton/pitonner/pitonnage
Forget nails, screws and hiking… here, **a piton** is the button you press on to make something, such as a television or a computer, work, as in **pèse su'l piton.** As a result, **pitonner** means "to tap" repeatedly, as in **y pâsse son temps à pitonner sur l'ordinateur.**

The word **piton** is also used in an expression that has nothing to do with buttons:

être de bonne heure su'l piton
to wake up early

planche
À' planche translates as "thoroughly" or "in depth," as in **si j'veux réussir mon examen, vâ falloir que j'étudie à' planche.**

pratique/pratiquer

A pratique is a "practice"; **pratiquer** means "to practice." As for the **coup de pratique**, it refers to a "first attempt."

râser

In addition to "shaving," this means "to come close," as in **ch'te dzi qu'ça' râsé!**

rejoindre

As for many other verbs, all you need to do is remove the initial R to figure out its meaning:

As-tsu réussi à le r'joindre?
Did you manage to reach him?

J'ai bein d'là misère à r'joindre les deux bouts.
I have a hard time making ends meet.

rendu

When you're **rendu**, you've arrived. However, the sentence **y'é rendu 5 heures** translates as "It's already five o'clock."

rentrer

Once again, the initial-R rule applies: **rentrer** is the same as entrer.

Other Words and Expressions

serrer
Québécois French uses this verb to mean "to put away."

suce/sucette/suçon
A **suce** is a "pacifier" and, contrary to Europe, a **sucette** is a "hickey" and a **suçon** is a "lollipop."

tétine
A **tétine** is the nipple of a bottle instead of a "pacifier" in Europe.

traite
The Québec meaning of this word is inspired by the English "to treat," as in **payer la traite à quelqu'un**.

A FEW REGIONAL EXPRESSIONS

ACADIA

aouindre
to remove

arruchemanganes
exaggerations

assaye
trial, court date

aviser
to see

bagoulard(e)
blabbermouth

baillarge
barley

basîr
to disappear

baye à laver
laundry vat

béler
to bail

bénaise
happy, content

bessons
twins

boire un coup à la grande tasse
to get drunk

(raconter des) brayonnages
to say incomprehensible/complicated things

brayonner
to ruin something/to dress badly

brochure
sweater

calouetter
to answer

clayon
gate

déconforter
to become discouraged

136

espérez-moi un p'tit élan
wait for me

fayot
edible part of the bean

(se) fiérer
to groom oneself

ginguer
to play

haim
(fish) hook

haut du jour
noon

hucher
to call out for someone

marionnette
Aurora Borealis

mitan
middle, centre

noroît
wind from the northwest

Other Words and Expressions

paré
ready

passe-pierre
edible sea plant

pichets de bouchure
fence posts

pijoune
hot beverage consisting of herbs and medicinal roots

pijouner
to cure someone with pijoune

pilot
pile

ragorner
to trim the grass around a tree by hand

vigneau
table used to dry cod

violon
tamarack

zeux/zeuces
those/the people

(avoir) zire de quelque chose
to be disgusted by something

THE PRAIRIES

abominable
extraordinary

abrier
to cover with a blanket

adon
coincidence

amanchure
problem

arabe
maple tree

arranger
to castrate

atouisteaux
belongings

bardasser
to shake up

bavasseux
a gossip

bazou
car

beau dommage
certainly

(faire le) berdas
to clean one's house

berdasser
to make noise/to make a mess

braquer
to abandon

(faire de la) broue
to brag

(se) canter
to go to bed

chambranler
to wobble

chaudasse
drunk

(faire les) combinages
to harvest the fields

crochir
to curve

cutter
sled (like the one used by Santa Claus)

écornifler
to spy

(s')épivardir
to boast

frais-chié
pretentious

galvauder
to tease/to gather/to reprimand/to loiter

godendard
two-person saw

gribouille
misunderstanding

gumbo
muddy soil

Other Words and Expressions

(avoir) mal aux cheveux
to be hungover

micouenne
ladle

nique
nest

pacté comme un œuf
drunk

phôner
to phone

piquette
local wine

quindre
to hold

rabiole
turnip

ravauder
to make a mess/to wander aimlessly

sciau
bucket

(avoir un) scrape
to come to blows

(être en) scrape
to quarrel

soincer
to chastise

stouque
haystack

tarauder
to screw on

tortue
pot-bellied stove

(être entre deux) tracks
to hesitate

(faire le) train
to take care of the cattle/to clean one's house

Other Words and Expressions

INDEX

CANADIAN FRENCH

149 Index

ENGLISH

Index

154